YOU'RE HIRED!
ASSESSMENT CENTRES

YOU'RE HIRED!
ASSESSMENT CENTRES
ESSENTIAL ADVICE FOR PEAK PERFORMANCE

CERI RODERICK

You're Hired! Assessment Centres: Essential Advice for Peak Performance

This first edition published in 2011 by Trotman Publishing, an imprint of Crimson Publishing, Westminster House, Kew Road, Richmond, Surrey TW9 2ND

© Trotman Publishing 2011

Author Ceri Roderick

British Library Cataloguing in Publication Data
A catalogue record for this book is available from the British Library

ISBN: 978 1 84455 378 5

Typeset by RefineCatch Ltd, Bungay, Suffolk
Printed and bound by Ashford Colour Press, Gosport, Hants

Acknowledgements

With thanks to all my colleagues at Pearn Kandola for their patience as I prepared this book and to all my clients over the years who provided the experience on which this book is based.

I dedicate this book to Nia, Megan and Tim who have probably taught me more psychology than anyone else!

CONTENTS

LIST OF ACTIVITIES

ABOUT THE AUTHOR

Ceri Roderick is a business psychologist and one of the UK's most experienced experts on assessment centre design and delivery. He designed his first assessment centre in 1985 and has since designed assessment processes for many of the UK's largest organisations – in the public and private sectors. As well as training assessors, he has himself been an assessor in hundreds of assessment centres, involving thousands of candidates.

Starting his career as a lecturer in applied psychology, Ceri has been consulting in commerce, industry and for government departments for over 25 years. This experience, together with his work in coaching, advising and supporting people about to attend an assessment centre, is all brought together in this book.

INTRODUCTION

Assessment centres are possibly the most daunting form of selection and assessment that most of us will face, yet they don't need to be.

I went through my first assessment centre 30 years ago and in writing this book I have tried to incorporate the advice and guidance I wish I had had in advance of the two days I spent locked up in the Old Admiralty Building attending what used to be called the Civil Service Selection Board.

I have spent much of my working life delivering and designing assessment centres for a wide range of public and private sector organisations at all levels, from initial entry up to board appointments. That experience has shown that there are definite techniques and tools that you can apply to make sure you perform at your best during an assessment centre. I have distilled that knowledge and experience here to give you the best possible chance to shine during the variety of typical assessment centre exercises. The principles and examples provided apply to the whole range of selection and assessment situations in which assessment centres are used (including development centres, a variation on the assessment centre theme, where the data gathered is used for development and training purposes rather than for pure selection).

Assessment centres are multiple assessment events containing a variety of different exercises, tests and simulations so that a potential employer can get the fullest possible picture of your performance. The full range of assessment centre exercises and activities will be covered in this book, though other books in this series, for example *You're Hired! Interview Answers* and *You're Hired! Psychometric Tests*, give still more detail about these specific selection methods.

Forewarned is forearmed and the examples and guidance provided here will demystify the assessment centre process and help to make sure that you are in the best possible shape to demonstrate your full range of talents and abilities to your future employer.

The good news is that if you have been asked to attend an assessment centre, you have already made it on to a pretty short shortlist; let's make sure that you fully exploit the opportunity!

HOW TO GET THE BEST FROM THIS BOOK

This book can be navigated in different ways so you can use it in whatever way suits your preferred learning style. If you are practically minded or if you already know the kinds of exercise you will be facing in your assessment centre, then you might want to go straight to the sections containing examples of different exercises and simulations (see Chapters 4–8). If, on the other hand, you want to understand the principles on which assessment centres are built, how they are structured and how the assessors/observers are operating, then the earlier chapters in this book will give you the information you need.

To help you decide where you want to start, here is a brief synopsis of each chapter.

Chapter 1: a brief explanation of what an assessment centre is, why businesses use them and what exactly it is that they are measuring.

Chapter 2: the structure and content of a typical assessment centre, including a 'walk-through' from both the assessors' point of view and from your point of view as a participant. This chapter also introduces the all important 'assessment matrix' and gives you an overview of all the different exercises you might encounter.

Chapter 3: how to prepare yourself to do your best: including some basic homework that you can do and some personal preparation that will help to get you 'fit' for the assessment centre.

Chapters 4–8: multiple examples of assessment centre exercises and simulations to help you practise and prepare.

Chapter 9: troubleshooting, exploding some common myths and preconceptions and answering your FAQs.

1 AN INTRODUCTION TO ASSESSMENT CENTRES – THE BASICS

This chapter gives you a complete introduction to assessment centres. After reading it you will better understand:

■ what they are

■ how they are used

■ the criteria for doing well.

What are they?

An assessment centre is the name given to a particular kind of selection testing process that involves you, the candidate, in experiencing a combination of different exercises, simulations, tests and/or interviews as a way of showing how well you match the employer's needs. The key difference between this and a more traditional selection process is that the assessment centre gives the assessors the chance to actually observe your behaviour in relevant situations rather than just rely on what you tell them. So, for example, if the employer wants to know how well you might handle a situation where you had to deal with an unhappy customer, why not simulate that situation and see how you get on. An assessment centre is the decathlon of selection systems: you need to be able to shine across a range of disciplines.

The earliest use of this approach, namely asking candidates to undertake multiple exercises, was in the military (both in the UK and in the US). Post-war the approach was increasingly taken up by the Civil Service and by private industry, to the point that nowadays most medium and large employers use assessment centres for at least part of their recruitment and selection processes.

The assessment centre is a process not a place. The basic idea is that by observing how you perform in a range of different (but relevant) situations, the employer can get a much more rounded picture of your capabilities and your style.

In practical terms they usually run over one or two days, involve several applicants/candidates being assessed at the same time and involve several assessors observing you and combining the results of their evaluation. They can take place in a wide variety of locations but hotels, purpose-built conference venues or the employers' own premises are the most common.

Research shows that the information gathered during an assessment centre allows an organisation to make a much better prediction of how likely a candidate is to be successful in a job as compared to an interview alone. In an idealised situation, an organisation could try out all the available candidates for six months, carefully monitoring their performance and then finally appointing the one who does best. There are pretty obvious reasons why this is not practical, so the next best thing is to try and squeeze a range of job-relevant situations into a one- or two-day assessment centre so as to get the best possible sample of behaviour in a relatively short time.

When can you expect to encounter them?

An assessment centre is usually used towards the end of a selection process (not least because they are quite expensive for an organisation to set up and run), so if you have made it this far you are already on a fairly short shortlist, which is all the more reason to make sure that you are in good shape to give your best performance during the assessment centre itself.

If the organisation you are applying to has multiple vacancies (often the case during graduate recruitment for example), then you can look on the assessment centre as the final screening process – in other words more than one of the participants you go through the assessment centre with will get through. In the same way, if an organisation is using an assessment centre as an internal process, for example to assess suitability for promotion, then the result will often not simply be pass or fail. Rather, the information gathered during the assessment centre will be used to assess your suitability for a particular role or how ready you are for immediate promotion as opposed to needing some more experience or further training before they consider you to be ready.

Multiple exercises, multiple assessors, multiple criteria

Another way of looking at an assessment centre is as a process for getting the best possible sample of your skills and behaviour in the shortest possible time. To this end you are asked to take part in a range of activities (to get a sample of your behaviour in different situations) while being observed by more than one assessor (so that no one person's opinion can predominate) so as to assess you against a number of different competencies or criteria.

Competencies

Most organisations using assessment centres will be assessing you against their own competencies: these are criteria that they have researched and which they believe define effective performance in a particular role. To do well at an assessment centre it helps to understand competencies, as the whole centre will have been designed around them. Competencies are more than just a definition of specific skills, they are usually concerned with 'how' you do things and not just 'what' you do. For example:

- 'producing monthly accounts' is a skill or a duty required in a particular job. It is a specific set of steps and procedures
- 'accurate collation and interpretation of financial information' is a competence. It is broader than just the specific skill; it could be applied to more than the specific requirement of producing the monthly accounts.

Businesses design competencies to be specific and accurate, but general enough so that they can be applied across a range of jobs in the organisation. It is also worth remembering that a lot of organisations have a competency framework that is interpreted differently at different organisational 'levels'. For example, at a relatively junior level, the competency 'planning and organising' might be defined in terms of personal organisation, structuring your workload, maintaining records. At a more senior level 'planning and organising' is more likely to be defined in terms of coordinating the activities of large numbers of people, thinking much more long term about resources and so on. Clearly, it pays to have a good understanding of the level at which you are being assessed.

'STRETCH' COMPETENCIES

If you are going to take part in an assessment centre, it will often be the case that the role you are applying for represents a promotion or a 'stretch' from your current role. Make sure that you are thinking about what the competency looks like at the level above the role in which you are currently operating. Look at the job description and consider how it is different from your current role. Another approach is to think about your boss's role and responsibilities – how is it different from your own? It is all too easy to use your current experience and level of competence as your benchmark and this is a mistake. A significant promotion or change of role will not mean just doing more of the same but at a higher level. There will be qualitative as well as quantitative differences in what is expected of you and it is well worth exploring these differences in advance.

Competencies are typically drawn together in what is known as a 'competency model'. This is simply a list of competencies, together with definitions and examples, which clearly explain what outstanding performance would look like. Typically, organisations have between seven to nine competencies, and it is against these that you will be assessed during an assessment centre. The list of competencies that follows is generic but quite typical of the criteria that organisations use during assessment centres. It is worth having a close look at them because they will be used as the foundation for all the example material later in the book.

A TYPICAL LIST OF COMPETENCIES
- Planning and organising
- Creativity and innovation
- Team leadership
- Achievement oriented
- Analytical thinking
- Influencing and persuading
- Energy and drive
- Judgement and decision making
- Motivating others

This is a pretty comprehensive list of attributes and they are generic enough that I would say that if you were showing competence in all of these you would be a pretty impressive candidate!

Competencies that you encounter in applying for jobs may well have different names to the ones listed above because they are supposed to be organisationally specific, helping to define 'what it takes to be effective around here'.

Simplifying competencies

A whole competency framework is a lot to take in and hold in your head, especially when you are under pressure during an assessment centre. In fact, I would advise against trying to tailor your words or actions to specific competencies during an assessment centre or you will end up tying yourself in knots! The good news is that when you analyse a wide range of competency frameworks, there are predictable clusters of competencies that can make your job a lot easier. Most competency models can be collapsed (or clustered) into three broader areas, which gives you a very useful shorthand for understanding the competencies of an organisation much more easily. These three areas are described below.

CLUSTERING COMPETENCIES – THE 'TASK, THOUGHT, PEOPLE' MODEL

■ **Task** competencies are about delivering/completing tasks, setting objectives, getting things done.
■ **Thought** competencies are about the thinking elements such as problem solving, creativity, setting a direction, etc.
■ **People** competencies are about the people things, communicating, motivating, developing.

Almost all jobs will require elements from each of these three areas. Very few jobs are purely about task delivery, there are bound to be 'people' and 'thought' elements involved. In the same way, very few jobs would allow you to focus exclusively on 'thought' to the exclusion of all else – you will also have to talk to people, and deliver something. I call this model the Leadership Radar™, because like steering a ship or flying a plane you need to keep your eyes on all the radar screens if you want to navigate a safe course. Sometimes you'll need to focus on just one screen, at other times all three screens need to be taken into account. In an assessment centre, some exercises or activities may focus on one of these clusters specifically, but most will be seeking evidence of competencies from more than one cluster.

Taking the example competencies from above, I have clustered them for you into the 'task', 'thought' and 'people' categories below.

Task	Thought	People
Energy and drive	Judgement and decision making	Motivating others
Achievement oriented	Analytical thinking	Influencing and persuading
Planning and organising	Creativity and innovation	Team leadership

UNDERSTANDING AND SIMPLIFYING COMPETENCIES

If you are in the process of applying for a specific job or if you have already been invited to an assessment centre, chances are you have already seen the criteria or the competencies that your prospective employer is interested in. These might be in the form of a clear competency list or they might be presented as the 'qualities' that the employer is looking for. Look through their list and try classifying them under the following headings.

Task attributes:

Thought attributes:

People attributes:

I will return to this model in more detail in Chapter 2 when I look at the assessment matrix – a key tool for you to understand and use as part of your preparation for an assessment centre. However, it is useful to be aware of this three cluster model now so that you can start to think about how to do your own clustering based on the job description for the post you are applying for. This task becomes even easier if the organisation shares its competencies with you; it's worth checking any preparation material that you have been sent to see if they have been explicit about the competencies you are going to be assessed against.

IN A NUTSHELL

- Assessment centres use multiple assessors and multiple exercises to assess multiple criteria.
- Understanding competencies is an important step in performing well.
- You need to think about your performance as a whole across a range of competencies and exercises.
- You can simplify competencies by using the task, thought, people model as a way of ensuring that you are focusing on the relevant behaviours.

2 ASSESSMENT CENTRES – TYPICAL STRUCTURE AND CONTENT

If you have never been through an assessment centre before, what can you expect? This chapter will explain the structure and content of a typical assessment centre and will also walk you through a one-day assessment centre in detail, a blow-by-blow account, so that you can better picture the whole process. It covers:

- types of assessment centre

- typical assessment centre exercises

- case study – the candidate's view

- the assessment matrix

- behavioural indicators.

Types of assessment centre

There are a number of important ways in which assessment centres vary and some of these have implications for the way you prepare yourself and how you can maximise your chances of giving your best. The kind of assessment centre covered in this book is the most typical design and the aim is to give you examples of the most typical exercises you will come across. This said, there are some weird and wonderful variations on the assessment centre theme; at the extreme you can consider the TV programme *The Apprentice* to be an extended assessment centre with a strong sales focus.

Some of the more unusual assessment centre exercises or simulations arise from organisations' need to assess very specific aptitudes, abilities or even physical characteristics. So, for example, applicants for roles which have physical demands (e.g. the police or the fire service) can expect there to be an element of the assessment which is about their basic levels of fitness or physical capability. Unsurprisingly, entry into pilot training will contain measurement of things like reaction time and visual acuity as well as aspects of manual dexterity and spatial awareness.

These are specialised situations, however, and even in these situations, the majority of the assessment time will be given over to measuring broader aspects of your behaviour – in other words generic competencies such as interpersonal skills, problem-solving style and leadership characteristics (as outlined in Chapter 1).

Any specialist areas of assessment like these will be highlighted in the briefing material you receive in advance of any assessment centre.

EXPECT SOME FORMALITY

An assessment centre can seem a very formal process. Organisations vary in terms of how 'relaxed' they are willing to be in administering an assessment centre but a degree of formality and rigour is inevitable given the need to ensure that applicants receive the same treatment and the same chance to show what they can do. Don't let this put you off.

Pure assessment centre vs development centre

Sometimes, especially if the event is an internal process, you might find yourself being invited to a development centre. There are differences in emphasis between these processes though it is worth recognising that there is no hard and fast line between them. In essence, the distinction is in terms of how the information gathered at the centre is used. In a pure assessment centre the information gathered is simply used to support a decision to hire or appoint someone (or sometimes to decide who will join a particular pool of employees such as a 'high potential' group). In a pure development centre the information is used to support the individual's training or development, and there is no selection decision involved. Some of the other main differences are described below.

Assessment centre	Development centre
Focus on measurement – little or no feedback at the event	Focus on diagnostics – much more feedback in 'real time' at the event
Less transparency about the criteria or competencies	More transparency about the criteria or competencies
Outcome is a pass/fail selection decision	Outcome is a development or coaching plan identifying strengths and weaknesses
Tend to be more formal, for example no dialogue with assessors during the centre	Can be less formal, time for conversation with assessors/coaches
Written report outputs are aimed mostly at the employer to assist in decision making	Written report outputs are for the employer and the participant to drive development actions and training

Duration

Historically it was not uncommon for assessment centres to run over three or even four days. These days it is unusual to encounter an assessment centre of longer than two days and one day is even more common.

From your point of view as a participant in an event, the duration has some implications for the pace of the process and how you manage your own energy levels across the event. In a two-day process it will not be helpful if you have run out of steam at the end of day one!

At the same time, the shorter the event, the more concentrated it will be in terms of how much is being assessed and how quickly. A short event will give you less time to warm up to the exercises; therefore if you have a poor exercise for some reason, there will be less chance that you can redeem yourself. As you will see in the next section, part of the point of an assessment centre is that important characteristics will be observed and assessed more than once but this coverage will be reduced in a short centre: all the more important then that you can hit the ground with your feet running. See Chapter 3 for more on how to prepare.

Scenario-based designs

One of the advantages of an assessment centre is its ability to simulate real work situations. To this end, a lot of well-designed assessment centres will wrap up all the various exercises in one overall scenario, for example a fictitious company, so that you only have to absorb the background material once rather than having to imagine yourself into a different setting for each exercise. This kind of 'immersive' design aims to make it easier for you to throw yourself into the exercises and treat them as 'real'.

The trick is to go with the scenario and imagine yourself working within the fictitious company or department. You will usually have been given time to absorb the background material; this might include a short company history, an organisation chart, a list of key products, information about key customers and so on. The more you can identify with this information, the better placed you will be to use it appropriately in the exercises.

Typical assessment centre exercises

There are a wide variety of exercises that you might encounter as part of an assessment centre – limited only by the richness of the imagination of the exercise designers! The most typically encountered exercises do fall into distinct groups, however, and this section outlines the exercises that you are most likely to meet. Detailed examples follow in Chapters 4–8.

Interviews

Assessment centres often (but not always) contain an interview section. It is increasingly common for an interview to be done separately from the assessment centre itself but they are sometimes built in to the schedule.

In a competency-based interview you can expect the questions to be very focused, typically asking you to give an example of a time when you have had to display a certain kind of competency or capability. For example:

"Can you tell me about a time when you have had to show a lot of tenacity and resilience in order to achieve your objective?"

The interviewer is looking for a real example and you can expect there to be a number of follow-up questions to assess exactly what it was that you did and what the outcome was. This interview might last for as long as an hour but more typically, if it is embedded as part of the assessment centre, it will take about 40 minutes.

Much more information about competency-based interviews and how to do your best in them can be found in the book *You're Hired! Interview Answers: Impressive answers to tough questions* in the same series.

Psychometric tests

It is more common these days for psychometric tests (tests of your abilities aptitudes, preferences or 'style') to be administered separately from the assessment centre itself. Some assessment centres do incorporate them, however, and the results can either be used separately or, as before, the results will be incorporated into the assessment matrix in the usual way.

There is a difference in the way that ability tests and personality/preference/ style tests are usually used as part of the assessment process. Most often an ability test, for example how well you work with numbers or how well you solve verbal problems, will have been used as part of an initial screening process. Why after all would they put you through an expensive assessment centre if you were going to fail to meet the standard on a relatively cheap numerical reasoning test? Preference or style tests do sometimes get factored in to the assessment matrix, usually by looking at particular scales on the test to see whether they offer positive or negative evidence in relation to specific competencies. Indeed some of the most recent personality measures will give a direct indication in terms of particular competencies.

The aim of this book is to cover the most typically used exercises and processes, so psychometric tests are not included as part of the matrix, but there are one or two pointers about psychometric tests that are worth considering.

The main differences between ability tests and preference tests are shown in the table below.

Ability tests	Preference tests
Includes reasoning with numbers, words or diagrams	Includes personality, values and integrity questionnaires
There are absolute right and wrong answers	There is no 'correct' answer
Usually have a time limit	Are generally untimed

Tests are covered in more detail in the practice examples section (see Chapter 4) but a much more comprehensive account and many more practice examples can be found in the book *You're Hired! Psychometric Tests* in this series.

Role plays – simulated meetings

Role play exercises are very commonly used as part of assessment centres. Designers like them because, if they are well designed and well delivered, they can be used to simulate realistic job-related situations. This lets the assessors see how you behave in a relevant situation. The most typical role play simulations you will encounter include:

- a meeting with an unhappy customer or member of the public to deal with a complaint or issue
- a meeting with a member of staff to resolve a performance issue
- a fact finding meeting to explore someone else's view of an issue or gather relevant information from them
- a business development or sales-based meeting
- a meeting where you have to influence someone more senior than you in the organisation
- a meeting where you have to negotiate or bargain to get to the best possible outcome.

For some organisations these role plays can become very specific and very structured. These are usually used in settings where there are very clear dos and don'ts about how you must behave in a particular situation. Examples of this include the Prison Service and the Police Service. In this kind of assessment role play you will usually be given very clear guidance about how you are expected to behave.

The more general (and more typical) kind of role play is more likely to focus on your interpersonal skills and how well you are able to respond to people 'in the moment'. Sometimes assessors will be used to 'play' the part of the protagonist in a role play situation but more commonly in well-designed assessment centres, professional actors are used because of the greater realism and consistency they can bring to the exercise.

A lot of people find role play exercises particularly daunting, but there is no reason for this if you follow the tips and guidance provided in the examples section of this book. See Chapter 5 for more on role plays.

In-tray or inbox exercises

These are a tried and trusted element of a lot of assessment centres and they are designed to simulate the activity of sorting through a sheaf of material and deciding how to act on the information you have been given. Assessment centre designers like them because of their versatility, several issues can be contained in the same exercise and it provides a good insight to thinking, problem-solving and decision-making style.

The exercise can be presented, almost literally, as an in tray containing several folders or sheets of paper, or it can be presented electronically as a series of emails. The task is the same in both cases, read through the material, sort it in terms of what is important, urgent or both and then produce your responses in the form of letters, memos or further emails.

This kind of exercise can be bought off the shelf or, as is the case in more sophisticated assessment centres, can be purpose designed to reflect the organisation and role that the assessment centre is being used for.

In general they will contain a mix of tasks, for example:

- two or three (or more) items relating to the same issue where you have to consider all the information before making your response
- one-off items, for example a letter of complaint, where you are expected to quickly draft a response
- items relating to a potential conflict or dilemma which you have to resolve based on your experience, common sense and the available information
- data to be checked or to be acted upon.

Typically, assessors are looking for how well you can sort, prioritise, identify relevant information and then produce an appropriate response. See Chapter 8 for more on in-tray exercises.

Presentation exercises

Assessors are often interested in how well you can communicate and present an argument and presentation exercises are an obvious vehicle for this. Sometimes you will be asked to present on a topic that you have prepared in advance but it is also quite common for you to be asked to present based on information that you have received during the assessment centre itself. For example, to present your conclusions resulting from a case study (see below). Because of the timetabling of a typical assessment centre, presentations will usually be quite short (10 to 15 minutes) so being able to get your points across succinctly and clearly is important. As you will see in the examples chapters, presentation exercises can be problematic, not least because assessors will be trying to evaluate content as well as your presentation skill. However, the good news is that structure and practice can make a big difference to how well you come across in such exercises.

A variation on the presentation theme is group presentation exercises. Here you will be asked to present as part of a group, typically three or four, usually to communicate the results of a group task that you have been involved in. For example, you might have been asked to take part in a group discussion exercise and then, as a group, to present back your conclusions. In these circumstances the assessors will usually take pains to ensure that all the group members are involved in the presentation and/or will direct questions at individual group members at the end of the exercise. See Chapter 7 for more on presentation exercises.

Group exercises

Meetings are a common enough aspect of business life and therefore group exercises, usually simulating a meeting of some kind, are a very common feature of assessment centres. Clearly the assessors will be interested in how well you communicate and behave in this setting but they will also be looking at how you handle information or how good your ideas are as part of the exercise. The exercises can vary slightly in their set-up as follows.

- **Open-ended group exercises.** All members of the group will be given the same short brief or topic to discuss.
- **Assigned role group exercises.** As above except that one group member in turn will be asked to lead or 'chair' the discussion.

■ **Information-sharing group discussion.** Here, while all group members have the same basic brief, each person has additional or slightly varying information to bring to the table as part of the discussion.

■ **Conflicting information or agenda group discussion.** Here each member of the group is asked to debate or argue from a slightly different viewpoint. For example, it may be a discussion about who to appoint to a particular job and each of you may have been asked to argue the case for a particular candidate based on background information you have been given.

You may occasionally encounter a discussion that also contains elements of role play. For example, designers may include an actor or actors as part of the group discussion in order to see how well the group handles a disruptive colleague or someone who has a very different viewpoint.

The important thing to remember is that group discussion exercises are always about more than simply who does the most talking or who leads the discussion. See Chapter 6 for more on group exercises.

Case studies and analytical exercises

These exercises are sometimes built in as an element of an in-tray exercise (see above) but it is also quite common for them to appear as a standalone exercise. Their common feature is that they are usually data intensive. They ask you to absorb a lot of information and then to draw conclusions or make recommendations as a result.

The most common format is that you will be given a sheaf of relevant documents and an instruction to produce a short report outlining your recommendations. It is becoming more common for these exercises to be presented electronically, for example asking you to use real or simulated websites as part of the information you are asked to consider.

Fairly obviously these exercises are often focused on how well you handle data, how well you can analyse numerical information in a business format and how clearly you can turn this into a set of clear recommendations. They are frequently used in contexts where there is specific expertise that the assessors want to evaluate. For example, for finance or other roles where they need to know that you are able to apply a specific body of knowledge. So, as well as testing whether you can handle the information they give you, they are often looking to see if you can draw sound conclusions and come to reasoned judgements in a particular expertise area. Tips on handling this kind of exercise are included in Chapter 7.

ACTIVITY 2

GETTING FAMILIAR WITH EXERCISES

Having gained an understanding of the kinds of exercise that assessment centre designers use, read through any prework you have been sent in advance of an assessment centre and identify the kind of exercise you are most likely to encounter. This will help you to focus your preparation.

Type of exercise	Tick those you are likely to encounter
Interviews	
Psychometric tests	
Role plays – simulated meetings	
In-tray or inbox exercises	
Presentation exercises	
Group exercises	
Case studies and analytical exercises	

Integrated assessment centres

It is increasingly common for assessment centres to be built around a consistent theme or scenario: in other words, all the exercises will be built around the same situation, business or department. This is so that you can absorb one set of background briefing material that will then be relevant to the whole of the assessment centre. This approach also helps you to get your head around the relevant issues in a more holistic way and gives the assessors the chance to see if you are able to make links between the different elements of the assessment centre.

ASSESSMENT CENTRE WALK-THROUGH

A few weeks ago you applied for the role of assistant purchasing manager at Newco Foods Ltd and after an initial interview you have been invited to attend an assessment centre.

You arrive at the Bear Hotel at 8.30a.m., well ahead of the 9a.m. start time you were given in your joining instructions and are shown to a lounge area where you are asked to wait. The assessment centre administrator explains that there will be a short briefing at 9a.m and in the meantime to help yourself to tea and coffee.

At 9a.m. the assessment centre administrator invites you all to come into the main meeting room (there are eight of you all together) and the briefing starts. She explains the format for the day, saying that each of you will have a timetable and that you will often be doing different exercises at different times – except for the group discussion exercise which four of you will conduct at the same time. You are also introduced to the four assessors and it is explained that they will be observing you in the various exercises, interviewing you or marking any written output that you produce. You are then told that for the purposes of timetabling you are Candidate B and your timetable looks like this:

09.30	Preparation for group discussion exercise
10.00	Group discussion (with Candidates A, C and D)
11.00	Break
11.15	Personal interview
12.00	Preparation for role play 1 – Customer complaint
12.30	Lunch
13.00	Role play 1
13.45	Computer-based case study
15.00	Break
15.15	Preparation for role play 2 – Staff performance meeting
15.30	Role play 2
16.00	Debrief and close

As part of the briefing the administrator explains that during the interview you will also get feedback on the results of a personality questionnaire that you completed on-line about a week ago.

09.30

The administrator asks four of you to follow her into a smaller room and she explains that this is where you will prepare for the group discussion exercise. She gives you a short written brief that explains the background to the discussion, basically the four of you will have to agree (based on the information you have been given) the best way of organising the relocation of a small company to new premises. She tells you that you have half an hour, working alone, to familiarise yourself with all the information.

10.00

The administrator tells you that is the end of the preparation time. As she says this two of the assessors walk into the room and take up their seats in the corner of the room where they can see all four of you as you sit around a central table. One of the assessors asks if you have all understood the instructions and explains that they will be observing the exercise and that you should try to ignore them as much as you can – they will be taking no part in the discussion but will simply be observing and taking notes. The assessor says that the discussion can take up to 45 minutes and that you should manage the time yourselves though they will stop you if you start to overrun. He says 'you can start your discussion now' and off you go. After a few seconds of looking at each other, one of the other candidates speaks first and then you all join in.

Forty-five minutes goes by very quickly, it turns out that all four of you have the same basic brief but that each of you has additional information that is relevant to the discussion. It takes a while to get all the information together but once this has been done the discussion moves quickly to the best way of organising the relocation. You add your own ideas into the discussion and it seems to go well. You finish pretty close to time, the assessors say thank you (you managed to ignore them once the discussion started) then the administrator appears to take you back to the main room.

The administrator (who you now know to be Chris) tells you to grab a cup of coffee and that you have a one-to-one interview next.

11.15

The interview is with another of the assessors and it takes about 40 minutes. As well as asking about background and experience, most of the questions are about specific examples of how you have tackled different kinds of situations and, after a lot of probing and follow-up questions, you are ready for lunch!

12.00

But first you are taken back to the main room and told that you have half an hour to prepare for the exercise that you will be doing immediately after lunch. You are given a pack of background papers and you start to wade through them.

12.30

You have lunch back in the lounge area and you take the opportunity to catch up with some of the other candidates. It becomes apparent that you are all operating to slightly different timetables and that they have been asked not to discuss the details of the exercises they have completed so far. Even so, the conversation makes it clear that everyone recognises that the assessment centre is a rigorous and demanding process.

Lunch over, it's back to the next round of exercises.

13.00

The exercise you prepared before lunch is a role play; apparently you will be having a meeting with a professional actor who will be playing the part of a customer who is unhappy with the service they have received from Newco.

You are asked to go into a single meeting room where, predictably, one of the assessors is waiting for you. He explains that as soon as you are ready, the actor playing the part of the customer will come into the room and that you must handle the meeting from that point onwards. Once again, she points out that you should try to ignore the assessor and focus on conducting the meeting.

When the customer arrives he is unhappy rather than angry and you take the approach of asking lots of questions to make sure that you understand the complaint. It turns out that several deliveries from Newco have arrived late at the customer's stores, causing a lot of inconvenience to store staff; that there has been no apology or explanation for this. You take it on yourself to offer an apology and you promise that you will investigate the cause of the problem and reassure the customer that you will get back to them with an explanation. The meeting seems to have gone reasonably well and you are surprised how quickly you forgot that it was a role play and even that there was an assessor in the room!

At the end of the exercise the assessor takes you back to the main room where Chris is waiting for you. Three of the other candidates are already there and Chris starts the briefing for the case study exercise. She explains that you will have 1 hour 15 minutes to complete the exercise.

13.45

You are all seated in front of a separate laptop and Chris explains that each computer contains a number of emails relating to a number of different business issues. Your task is to read through them all and decide how you want to respond to them. She also makes the point that some of the emails might relate to the same issue so it is best to read through them all before you start responding. She makes sure that you all have the right opening screen in front of you and that you are all familiar with how to navigate through the emails and then she tells you to start.

A quick scroll through tells you that there are 17 email messages in total, some of them look relatively trivial but about ten of them seem to relate to three main issues. Each of these will require you to write a response. After about an hour you feel that you have covered the main issues, it has involved you writing five emails to tie up all the loose ends. You use the next ten minutes or so to go back over the exercise to make sure that you haven't missed anything.

15.15

After some coffee there is yet another role play and you are back in the main room preparing for it. This time the brief is quite short, 'a member of your team has asked for a meeting to discuss their promotion prospects and what they need to do to develop themselves in preparation for their next job'. The background information contains some memos from their previous manager and a couple of comments from HR. Not much to go on so you decide that you are going to have to spend a lot of the meeting exploring things with the person and then thinking on your feet in terms of any suggestions or ideas you put forward.

15.30

The set up is as before, the administrator takes you to a meeting room where the assessor is waiting, a couple of minutes later the role player arrives and the exercise starts.

The character you are meeting with seems quite withdrawn and the first five minutes is like getting blood out of a stone. Only by asking a lot of questions do you get to the point where some of the real issues start to come out. It seems that this person feels that they have been passed over for promotion and they are seriously thinking about leaving unless they get some clarity about what their prospects in the business are. It's a tricky conversation, and you are conscious that you don't want to make promises that you can't keep, but by the end of it you have at least got to the point where the person is going to go away and think about it and you are going to go away and explore the options in advance of meeting the person again at some future date. Not the most satisfying meeting but you do feel that you at least made some progress with the person concerned.

16.00

And suddenly you realise that that is it! You are back in the main room together with all the other candidates, it's 16.00. and Chris is starting the final de-brief. She thanks you all for your efforts, explains that all the assessors will now be meeting to collate their observations, and that she will be in touch over the next few days to offer feedback, explain the outcome and tell you what the next steps are.

So, there you have it: the assessment centre experience in 2,000 words!

The assessment matrix – it drives everything!

At the heart of all assessment centres is the assessment matrix; this is the grid that tells the assessors what is being observed/assessed in various exercises and how that information will be combined to reach a final decision. Understanding how this matrix works is a big advantage to you as a participant because it can provide some important clues as to how you can make the assessors' job easier, thus in turn making it easier for them to evaluate you positively. In some assessment centres the organisation might even share with you what this assessment matrix looks like, so check the preparation material they send you, but often they won't. The matrix helps you to think holistically about the assessment centre and this will help you to hone your performance.

THINK 'COMPETENCIES' NOT 'EXERCISE'

One of the big errors that people make as they go through an assessment centre is to assume, or think too simplistically about, what the assessors are looking for in a particular exercise. For example, 'this looks like a leadership exercise so I need to take charge, be directive and tell everyone what to do'. It is never as simple as this, at best you might miss the opportunity to demonstrate your abilities in other competencies that the exercise is measuring, and at worst you will overemphasise behaviours that the assessors will see as a serious negative.

The assessment matrix is developed in the following way:

- First, the organisation decided on the criteria/competencies that needed to be measured.
- Second, it decided on the kind of exercise or activity that would provide the best vehicle for revealing the presence or absence of that competency.
- Third, it designed (or had designed) the assessment matrix that matches competencies to exercises.
- Fourth, it got down to the detailed design of the exercises.

There are always compromises at the design stage. The constraints of time and resource mean that assessors are usually measuring more than one competency during a given exercise, there are seldom as many exercises as assessors would like to get multiple measures of everything, and time constraints mean that exercises often don't run for as long a period as assessors would ideally like.

The assessment matrix makes this set of compromises explicit so that the assessors can see where relevant information is coming from and how much weight to give to that information.

ACTIVITY 4

UNDERSTANDING THE ASSESSMENT MATRIX

Here is an example of an assessment matrix. It is based on the same competencies introduced in Chapter 1, and uses the exercises that were described in the 'walk-through' above. Critically, it shows which exercises measure which competencies.

	Interview	Group discussion exercise	Role play 1 – customer	Case study	Role play 2 – staff	Overall
Energy and drive		*			*	
Achievement orientated	*	*	*			
Planning and organising		*		*	*	
Judgement and decision making	*		*	*		
Analytical thinking	*			*		
Creativity and innovation			*	*		
Motivating others	*	*			*	
Influencing and persuading	*	*	*			
Team leadership		*			*	

The different grey shadings represent the task, thought, people competency clusters described in Chapter 1.

From this matrix, you can see that most of the competencies are measured three times, this is good news because it means that a less than optimum performance in any one exercise is unlikely to be a 'show stopper'.

You can also see that not every competency is measured in every exercise – this is good design practice and means that assessors will not be overloaded by trying to assess too many things at one time.

Still closer examination tells you that some exercises seem to be weighted towards particular kinds of competency. If you remember the clustering of competencies introduced in Chapter 1 (task, thought, people) then you can see that the case study exercise seems to be particularly important in terms of assessing the 'thought' cluster of competencies. At the same time, the group exercise seems to be particularly loaded towards the 'task' and 'people' clusters.

As a general rule of thumb, exercises that have a strong interactive element, such as group discussions or one-to-one role plays, will tend to major on 'people' competencies – no big surprise there. Exercises that require you to plan or to deliver something by a particular time will often major on 'task' competencies, and in this case the group discussion has a strong element of this. Exercises that require you to make decisions based on background information (often putting these decisions into written form) will usually be assessing a strong element of the 'thought' cluster, and in this example the case study exercise has this weighting.

By understanding the assessment matrix you can:

■ Recognise that multiple aspects of your 'style' are being measured in any given exercise. This means that you need to attend to all aspects of the task. For example, just performing in a very directive way during the group discussion might get you marks for 'energy and drive' and 'achievement orientated' but may leave you falling short in terms of 'motivating others'. Top tip here is don't try to second guess the exercise, try to think about the task as a whole rather than making an assumption about how they want you to behave.

■ Recognise that a poor performance in any one exercise is unlikely to damage your chances beyond repair. For example, a lot of people say that they do not perform well in role play exercises, or you may feel that you undersold yourself during the interview. The matrix tells you that there are opportunities to redeem yourself, so move on. Don't dwell on a poor exercise; instead focus on doing well in the next activity.

■ Recognise that the matrix tells you something about how the assessors are going about their job. They are aiming to get information about the 'real you' across competencies and across exercises. You can easily imagine that eight different candidates would produce eight very different patterns of scores across the matrix – reflecting their particular strengths and weaknesses. As well as overall scores (how highly you have rated against each competency) assessors will often be looking for patterns of scores.

Have a look at the following pattern: the ratings are based on a five point rating scale where 1 is low and 5 is high.

Candidate 1	Interview	Group discussion exercise	Role play 1 – customer	Case study	Role play 2 – staff	Overall
Energy and drive	3	2			3	3
Achievement orientated	3	2	4			3
Planning and organising		3		4	3	3
Judgement and decision making	2		4	3		3
Analytical thinking	4			5		5
Creativity and innovation			4	3		4
Motivating others	2	2			1	2
Influencing and persuading	3	2	3			2
Team leadership		1			2	2

Notice firstly that the assessors haven't simply averaged scores to come to their overall rating in the final column. Practice varies – sometimes they will apply a strict average but quite often they will look at the quality of the evidence from the various exercises and come to a view as to what score best reflects the evidence. That is what they have done here.

From this pattern you can see that this candidate seems to have done better in one particular exercise (the case study) and against one particular cluster of competencies, in this case the 'thought' cluster. In making a decision based on this information the assessors will be thinking about the job requirement and what this pattern means in terms of 'fit' with the job. This candidate seems to be analytical and task focused but perhaps not quite so strong in terms of people skills.

Clearly, as a candidate you will want to maximise your scores across all exercises and across all competencies, but it is worth recognising that a well-designed assessment centre is intended to help the assessors to differentiate between candidates on exactly this kind of basis. Chapter 3 will help you to think about your 'natural' style and how this can help you to anticipate those exercises and those competencies that play to your strengths or that represent more of a risk for you.

Behavioural indicators: what are they looking for?

It is worth considering the process that the assessors go through to come to their ratings. The important thing to recognise is that well-trained assessors will not just be relying on their own interpretation of what, for example, 'team leadership' looks like. They will be using **behavioural indicators** that guide them as they watch the exercises.

The actual steps that a well-trained assessor will be going through are as follows.

1. **Observe.** Closely watching the exercise in order to spot important behaviour.
2. **Record.** Making detailed notes of what they have actually seen.
3. **Classify.** Go back over their notes to identify which behaviours they observed 'belong' to which of the competencies they are assessing.
4. **Evaluate.** Look at the observed behaviours in terms of each competency and evaluate or rate them based on a set of behavioural indicators.
5. **Integrate.** Put all the ratings together to come to an overall decision as in the assessment matrix above.

The behavioural indicators that the assessors use are the means by which they turn an observation into a rating, so they are important!

Just as the competency framework will vary from organisation to organisation, then so will the specific behavioural indicators that assessors use to rate performance. However, there is enough commonality that it is possible to identify behaviour which is likely to serve you well in particular exercises. In the practice examples in Chapters 4–8 relevant behavioural indicators are identified to help you think through what it takes to do your best in each kind of exercise. Just to whet your appetite, however, here is a sample set of behavioural indicators. They relate to the competency 'team leadership' and they are specific to the group discussion exercise. This means that after you have completed the group discussion exercise, the assessor uses these indicators to decide how they are going to rate you in terms of team leadership.

Here are some examples of the kind of behavioural indicators that assessors are likely to be looking for.

Group discussion

Rating	Behavioural indicators	Comments
	• Contributes to establishing the group's plan	
	• Makes clear suggestions for how to complete the task	
	• Helps to manage the group, e.g. keeps track of time and progress	
	• Gives other people time to talk and contribute	
	• Actively brings other people into the discussion, doesn't ignore anyone	
	• Makes decisions but ensures there is consensus	
	• Consistently and actively helps the group to achieve the task	

OK, so now you know what an assessment centre looks and feels like as a whole, you have an understanding of the component parts of the process, and you have some insight in to what the assessors are doing as they observe and

BE YOURSELF – BUT ON A GOOD DAY!

It is best not to second guess the exercises and make assumptions about what the assessors are looking for, far better to be yourself rather than to pretend to adopt a style that doesn't suit you and that might not be what they want anyway. This said, you should be thinking about the likely behavioural indicators that the assessors are looking for in a particular situation. You won't know what they are in detail but it is helpful to think about the kinds of behaviour that are likely to be seen as positive or negative examples. There will be more about this in Chapter 3 on preparation, and in the examples in Chapters 4–8.

evaluate you during the assessment centre. Armed with this knowledge you are now ready to move on to consider the kind of preparation that will help to ensure that you shine!

IN A NUTSHELL

- Assessment centres are usually highly structured events and understanding how they work makes them a lot less daunting.
- The best way to think about the whole process, and each individual exercise, is as a series of opportunities.
- Take a close look at the briefing material you are sent in advance of the assessment centre, and explore it for clues about the competencies and the kinds of exercise that will be included.
- Bear in mind the assessment matrix that underpins the design of the assessment centre: it will help you to think about the process as a whole.
- Consider the behaviours and the behavioural indicators that assessors are likely to be looking for.

3 PREPARATION

Preparing for an assessment centre makes a significant difference to how well you are likely to perform. As well as helping you to anticipate the exercises and the criteria that you will be assessed against, preparation also helps your frame of mind. Most people are nervous about assessment centres and settling these nerves is an important benefit of your preparation.

This chapter will show you how to:

■ research the organisation and its selection criteria

■ understand your personal assets and risks in relation to the assessment process

■ gain an insight by seeing the process from the assessors' point of view.

Preparing for your assessment centre

If you have been invited to attend an assessment centre, the chances are you will have been through a couple of stages of selection already and that you will have learned something about the organisation as a result. In addition to what you already know you should check that, as a minimum, your preparation includes:

- researching the organisation and/or the department that you are applying to
- finding out as much as you can about their selection criteria/competencies
- finding out as much as you can about the assessment process itself (timing, structure, location, exercises)
- your own personal preparation; understanding your assets and risks in relation to the assessment centre and preparing yourself mentally.

Researching the business

There are several very good reasons for researching the organisation you are seeking to join.

- To ensure that this is a job you want in an environment where you can prosper and in a role that provides the prospects you are looking for.
- To ensure that you do everything you can to anticipate and prepare yourself mentally for the assessment exercises you will experience.
- To ensure that you can show an informed interest in the business, particularly important if the assessment centre contains an interview. Assessors will often take any lack of background research on your part as a lack of motivation for joining the organisation.
- To ensure that any apprehension you have is managed and does not get in the way of your performance during the assessment centre.

It's worth emphasising that most organisations will expect you to have done this research and will be disappointed if it becomes clear that you haven't. For example, if you are applying to a very sales-focused organisation, like a retailer, you can expect them to be interested in how you relate to customers or clients. You should expect that this might be one of the discussion topics you are given during, for instance, a group discussion exercise. So it makes sense for you to have done some reading around customer and retail issues as part of your preparation. If you fail to do this you will risk appearing to be poorly motivated for a career in retail!

Once again, I must stress that this is not about you second guessing the exercises or the assessment process. However, appearing to be well informed (not expert necessarily) is likely to impress the assessors.

Where to find information

The internet

A business's own website is the obvious first port of call to find out more about them and, potentially, about the job you have applied for. Your preparation should include more than just scanning through the site. It is worth making a specific note, actually writing down, information relating to:

- organisational structure and the names of key individuals, for example the CEO and the directors/senior managers of the part of the business you are applying to – you can usually find this information in the 'Our People' section of the website
- mission and values statements
- markets, products and services
- recent news and company press releases.

You might also find a section of the site relating to 'working with us' or 'current vacancies'. These are well worth looking at for examples of job descriptions and the kind of criteria that the business recruits against. You might even find the business' competencies (selection criteria) explicitly mentioned here.

USING CORPORATE WEBSITES

As an example of a large corporate website (and some of them do take some navigating) BT is quite typical. Starting from the home page you can follow the link to BT Group, then 'Explore BT PLC'. Here you will find information about the annual report, corporate news, podcasts. There is also a link to 'Current Jobs' and specifically a link to the BT Graduate Programme. On this page there is a section labelled 'videos' and within this you will find the BT Values listed, offering some important clues to their selection criteria. This kind of exploration is valuable regardless of whether you are applying for a graduate level job or a position that is more senior, the values are the same throughout the company.

As well as the business' own website, there are other websites that can also provide valuable information. If you do an internet search for your target organisation you will get a lot of hits in addition to the company's own website. These might include comments from business journalists, company histories on sites such as Wikipedia, or blog sites relating to the business. These will be less helpful in terms of any specifics about selection processes or criteria but can be very valuable in terms of background, market perceptions of the business, business trends and so on. It is not uncommon for assessment centres to have exercises, for example group discussions, where a good general knowledge of relevant business matters will help you to contribute and appear well informed.

Newspapers and magazines

Businesses and the people who work for them are always keenly aware of what is being said about them in the press and in the trade press. If you can research and use some of this information then it will put you in a good position to appear well informed.

For broad information about trends and wider market factors, *The Economist* is a particularly good source. They conduct regular sector reviews and these can give you a good overview of the kinds of issues that are of concern to senior managers/directors in the business you have applied to. It is also worth looking at the trade press for the relevant business sector: a little time spent reading *The Grocer* (retail), *Oil and Gas* (energy sector), *Accountancy Today* (business consulting) and similar journals can go a long way to acquainting you with the trends, the competitors and the relevant business language, particularly if you are applying for a job in a sector that is unfamiliar to you. Every sector has its own trade press and there is no better way of quickly familiarising yourself with anything from air conditioning (*HVP – Heating, Ventilation and Plumbing*) to insurance (*Insurance Age; Insurance Times*).

From the organisation itself

It is well worth asking the organisation for as much information as they are willing to provide. If you have been invited to an assessment centre you can expect to receive a briefing pack and at least basic joining instructions but there is no harm in asking if there is any other information available – be cheeky and ask if it is possible to see competencies or selection criteria, the worst that can happen is that they say no. Most organisations will be keen to show scrupulous fairness in terms of how all candidates are treated so don't be surprised if this limits the amount of information they are willing to share in advance.

At the end of all your research, you should aim to have assembled a portfolio of information that includes answers to the following questions:

■ What are the main business priorities at the moment?
■ How are they seen by the competition; by the staff; by the industry?
■ What are they famous/infamous for?
■ What do they hold up as their big successes or failures?
■ What kind of people get ahead in the organisation?
■ How are they the same or different from similar organisations?

The more you can find out, the better; it will help you to understand the context of the assessment centre you are attending. For example, knowing that the business you have applied to is expanding a number of its overseas offices will help you to understand why a number of issues relating to international and cultural matters appear in the in-tray exercise. It will also help you to quickly home in on 'hot topics' so that you can give them your full attention.

Researching the selection criteria

In an ideal world a business would tell you explicitly what the selection criteria for your chosen role are. In practice they often don't, so anything you can do to better understand what they are looking for will give you an edge. Even if you have not been told what the specific selection criteria are, you will often be sent or can access through their website (see above) information about company values or generic competencies that they look for in applicants. A typical list of organisational competencies could be as follows:

■ planning for success
■ strategic commercial thinking
■ innovation and change
■ leading successful teams
■ analysis and judgement
■ developing self and others
■ operational delivery.

The task, thought, people model introduced in Chapter 1 is a useful tool to understand and simplify this kind of competency list. Just to remind you:

- **Task competencies** are typically about operational delivery, results, implementation, plans, targets, getting things done.
- **Thought competencies** are typically about direction, strategy, creativity, problem solving, change, innovation, judgement, decision making.
- **People competencies** are typically about teams, collaboration, empathy, interpersonal skills, influencing, communication, personal development, motivation, coaching.

So the competencies listed above would be clustered in terms of the task, thought, people model as follows.

- Planning for success   Task
- Operational delivery   Task
- Strategic commercial thinking   Thought
- Innovation and change   Thought
- Analysis and judgement   Thought
- Developing self and others   People
- Leading successful teams   People

If you have access to the competencies in advance, you should prepare by doing this clustering for yourself. If you are only told about the competencies at the start of the assessment centre, by having the model in your head you can still quickly get a sense of the 'shape' of the exercises to help you to focus your performance. Holding on to three ideas – task, thought, people – is a lot easier than trying to memorise and then reference their whole competency framework in 'real time'. The reason for doing this is to help you remember that most exercises will contain elements from all three of the clusters – remembering all three aspects will help you to deliver a rounded performance. Let's look at an example of where this can make a real difference.

Here is an assessment matrix based on the competencies listed above; the order has been changed to reflect the clustering that you/I have done.

	Presentation	Group discussion exercise	Role play 1 – coaching	In-tray exercise	Role play 2 – supplier meeting	Overall
Planning for success	*	*			*	
Operational delivery		*	*		*	
Strategic commercial thinking	*			*		
Innovation and change	*			*	*	
Analysis and judgement		*	*	*		
Leading successful teams	*	*		*		
Developing self and others			*	*	*	

You can see that this matrix contains an in-tray exercise. These exercises tend to drive us to focus on 'task' and 'thought' behaviours. For example, we will typically spend most of our time making sure that our analysis is right, that we have spotted all the main issues and that we have drafted letters or responses that solve the problems that have been raised. It is very easy to forget that 'people' competencies might be relevant here as well, and in this exercise the two 'people' competencies are also being measured. Therefore, it might be that the assessors are paying particular attention to the tone of any letters you write, or are looking to see if you have thought through the team implications of the suggestions you are making. The task, thought, people model helps you to remember to think holistically. It pays to practise this in advance of the assessment centre (see Chapter 8 for a concrete example).

Here are some examples of typical organisational competencies that I have clustered for you:

Task	Thought	People
Sales focus	Change orientated	Team leadership
Planning and organising	Creativity and innovation	Collaborative working
Commitment to results	Strategic thinking	Engaging others
Energy and drive	Broad-based business thinking	Networking and communicating
Achievement orientated	Provides vision and direction	Emotional intelligence
Commercially driven	Creative problem solving	Empathy/developing rapport
Delivering results	Analytical thinking	Motivating others
Project planning	Thinks outside the box	Building and developing teams
Project management	Exploring new ideas	Influencing and persuading
Resource management	Inventive and imaginative	Teamworking
Target orientated	Judgement and decision making	Interpersonal skills

Researching the assessment centre itself

Most of your basic questions about the assessment centre should be answered as part of the briefing material you have received, for example location, duration, dress code and so on. It is good practice for the organisation to also give you some background about the kind of exercises you will be experiencing and you might well be asked to do some preparatory work in the form of completing tests or reading background material that is relevant to the exercises.

DRESSING THE PART!

Dress code: hopefully you will be given some guidance about how you are expected to present yourself at the assessment centre. For example, casual, smart casual, business dress and so on. As a general rule of thumb it is better to be too smart than to be too casual, so if in doubt always err on the side of over dressing.

The more you can find out the better, so if the organisation is not particularly forthcoming about the kinds of exercises or the competencies they will be assessing you against, then it is worth exploring other avenues to fill in these gaps. This is not cheating, it is simply getting yourself in the best possible shape to show them what you can do. If you were an athlete it would help you to know if you were going to be asked to take part in the 200 metres, the 800 metres or the long jump! Here are some things you can try.

■ Simply ask the person who has contacted you from the organisation – the worst that can happen is that they say no!
■ Do you know anyone who has applied to this organisation in the past? What was their experience of the assessment process? Don't ask them about the detail of exercises, because it won't help you, but understanding the broad scope of the exercises can help you to focus your preparation.
■ Go on-line. If the organisation you are applying to is a large one, chances are that there will be blogs or other commentaries on-line that could give you some clues.

Researching yourself: assets and risks

More so than for any other kind of assessment, time given to understanding yourself, your style and your assets/risks in relation to both the job and the assessment situation, is time very well spent. By assets I mean those characteristics, abilities and preferences that you can bank on to show yourself in a good light; by risks I mean those aspects of you which might not serve you so well in terms of the impact you have during an assessment centre.

It's surprising how many people have only a poor understanding of how they come across to others in different situations. I will cover the importance of personal impact more fully in the exercise practice chapters, but as part of your preparation it is worth checking that your own perception of your style is reasonably accurate.

People vary in terms of how self-aware they are so ask a few friends, colleagues or family members to give you their opinion about how they think you will come across in different situations. For example, you might describe to them the exercise outlines I have provided and then ask them what they think your strengths and weaknesses are likely to be in such situations.

They might tell you that you tend to talk very quickly when presenting, or that you tend to be quite modest when describing what you have done. Whatever the feedback, it will help you to check that your own view of yourself is accurate. Armed with this information you can then ask yourself about the likely impact of your style in different kinds of exercises:

"How confident do I sound when I am talking in a group?"

Research shows that interactive exercises such as group discussions often over-emphasise, and thus tend to put too much weight on, social confidence and verbal fluency. A good assessment centre will try and get beyond this by using behavioural indicators that are not just about how much or how assertively you talk.

Nevertheless, understanding how confident and fluent you typically sound is important. It's also worth remembering that for most people, nervousness has a dampening effect on normal levels of confidence and fluency. Sources you can use to assess this include your friends, feedback from previous assessments or interviews, your own knowledge of whether, for example, people typically see you as thoughtful and quiet or expressive and extravert.

Thinking about yourself objectively can be difficult – this is why you need to give time to this element of your preparation. How does your voice sound? How quickly do you speak? Do the words you use make you sound confident (too many positives risk making you sound arrogant)? Do the words you use make you sound too modest (too many negatives will make you appear to be self-doubting and uncertain)? A lot of people find this balance hard to achieve so do practise out loud.

"Are there any particular exercises that I think will be more of a challenge for me?"

I said earlier that a lot of people find role play exercises uncomfortable or even daunting. How do you feel about them? Do you find it easy to speak up and get your ideas across in a discussion or do you tend to be quieter, waiting for a gap in the conversation before you speak? Do you risk being over-talkative?

Introspection can only take you so far with understanding these aspects of your style. You need feedback from other people who know you well and you need to ask them to be really honest and objective with you. For most people, any feedback you get from asking these questions should be used to moderate any less helpful aspects of your style, not to try and change your style altogether. Radically changing your style is very difficult to do and 'being yourself' is an important aspect of doing well at an assessment centre. Even so, it helps to know if there are any strong aspects of your style that it would pay you to moderate a little. The time to practise this is in advance of the assessment centre otherwise you risk your impact being clunky, inconsistent and leaving the assessors suspicious about who the 'real you' is!

This is worth emphasising, because people tend to make the best impact at assessment centres when they appear authentic and 'comfortable in their own skins' so yes, prepare, but don't change anything that will get in the way of 'you' coming across as a real person.

"Do I have particular assets and risks in terms of the job and the competencies?"

At the very least, you will have been given a description of the role you have applied for, so even if you have little else to go on this will let you deduce some of the main competencies your prospective employer is interested in.

Your research into the competencies needed for the role comes into its own here. Again, I would suggest using the task, thought, people framework as a way of checking, in broad terms, how your experience, skills, competencies and personal attributes map on to the organisation's requirements. I have already looked at how to use this model during the assessment centre, but it is also worth using it as a way of getting a broad picture of where you are likely to be perceived as relatively strong or weak in terms of their criteria. So ask yourself the following questions.

"Am I likely to come over as a TASK person?"

"Do I have a preference for operational delivery and driving things through against deadlines?" "Do I find it easiest to talk about delivery, plans, and targets?" "Will I be prone to homing in on this aspect of any given exercise at the expense of other relevant areas?"

"Am I likely to come over as a THOUGHT person?"

"Do I enjoy and put a lot of emphasis on developing ideas or strategy?" "Do I find it easiest to talk about analysis, judgement and insight?" "Will I risk giving too much of my time during an exercise to making sure that I understand the facts, and analysing them rather than acting on them?"

"Am I likely to come over as a PEOPLE person?"

"Do I put a high value on teamwork and getting results through others and developing people?" "Do I find it easiest to talk about influencing, coaching, collaborating?" "Will I focus too much on keeping everyone happy at the expense of actually delivering a result?"

I said earlier that you need to remember to be yourself during an assessment centre but it is helpful to understand what **you** look like to other people!

For most of us, one or two of these areas tend to be more highly developed than the others, often because of our natural preferences or our experience. But it is worth giving some thought to how your natural preferences are likely to appear to assessors during an assessment centre. If, for example, your analysis tells you that you are most likely to impress assessors as a 'thought' person, with a strong second preference in terms of 'people', then you can shape your preparation to ensure that you take opportunities during the assessment centre to give attention to detailed implementation, meeting deadlines and delivering against obstacles so as to reinforce your 'task' abilities.

Understanding your assessors

You now have a good idea of the structure of an assessment centre and the kinds of exercise it is likely to contain, but it is also worth thinking through how your assessors are operating, the rules they are following and how to make their life easier.

Your assessors will have been trained and briefed to use competencies and behavioural indicators (as described on pages 34–35) but what does their day look like? Chapter 2 contained a candidate's eye view of the assessment centre but what does it look like from the assessor's point of view?

Depending on the design of the assessment centre, each assessor will be taking responsibility for two, three or four of the candidates. So, although they will not usually see these candidates in every exercise, they are responsible for pulling together all the information on these candidates. Typically the timetable

UNDERSTANDING YOUR ASSESSORS

You should not be surprised then if the assessors you meet are business-like rather than sociable. This can put some people off but don't read anything into it, they are simply busy. Don't expect them to give you much in the way of hints about how you are doing, because apart from being too busy, at this stage they simply won't know because all the information relating to you hasn't been pulled together yet. Just to give you some insight to this, here is the assessor's timetable for the assessment centre described in 'the walk-through'.

8.30	Arrival and briefing – allocation of candidates
9.00	Meet the candidates
9.30	Observe role play 1 – Candidate A
10.00	Observe group discussion – Candidates C and D
11.00	Write up and evaluation time
11.15	Interview Candidate B
12.00	Write up and evaluation time
12.30	Lunch
13.00	Observe role play 1 – Candidate B
13.30	Write up and evaluation time
13.45	Observe role play 2 – Candidate C
14.15	Write up and evaluation time – marking case study output for Candidates C and D
15.00	Break
15.30	Observe role play 2 – Candidate D
16.00	Assessors' meeting and integration of scores
18.00	Close

Not until all the exercises are completed and scored at 16.00 are the assessors in a position to compare notes with each other and fill in the assessment matrix for each candidate. This is often called the 'wash up meeting' and it is where the final pattern of your scores emerges.

will be arranged so that they see slightly more of these candidates than they do the others. What this means is that the assessors are busy! Having observed an exercise they will be using the behavioural indicators to reach their evaluation, but sometimes other exercises will intervene, meaning that they will be coming back to do the evaluation of a particular exercise some time later. For this reason their training will have put heavy emphasis on taking good notes rather than relying on their memories.

So, what can you do to make it easier for the assessors to do their job and see the best side of you?

- Be punctual and get to the right place at the right time. Even five minute overruns on time play havoc with the assessment centre timetable: remember that actors, assessors and candidates all have to be coordinated.
- Try to ignore them! This might sound odd but it is important that you try to ignore them as they are observing exercises, as it is off-putting for them and you if you are continually glancing at them to see what they are doing.
- Follow the exercise brief. In case study or in-tray exercises always produce your output in the format they ask for, marking time is short and you will not endear yourself to the assessor if they are having to try and make sense of output that doesn't fit the required pattern.
- Commit to the exercise and take it seriously. Assessors are disconcerted by (and will take a dim view of) anyone who is seen to be game playing or not making a serious attempt to throw themselves into the exercise. They probably don't have behavioural indicators for this so it makes their job more difficult and is unlikely to work in your favour.

RESPECT THE PROCESS

I once worked with a senior executive who kept failing assessment centres because he would not follow the 'rules' of exercises. For example, he would stop halfway through a group discussion exercise, turn to the assessors and say 'do we really need to go on with this – it's a pointless discussion?' In the same way he would pause in mid-stream during a role play exercise and say to the actor 'is there any point in me bringing up the next two issues, your brief probably doesn't cover them in enough detail?'. This was a highly intelligent man but he felt that he was 'above' the assessment process and the result was that he annoyed the assessors by making it hard for them to follow procedure in making their assessments. Needless to say he failed to get the jobs.

IN A NUTSHELL

- Preparation can make a real difference to how well you do at an assessment centre, the better prepared you are, the more quickly you will be able to take advantage of the opportunities that an assessment centre offers you to show what you can do.
- Research the organisation and/or the department. You don't need to be an expert but any general knowledge about the sector or the service your prospective employer offers will be helpful.
- Find out as much as you can about the company's selection criteria. Knowing what they are likely to be looking for makes it much easier for you to focus your preparation.
- Research the assessment centre itself – structure and content.
- Prepare yourself, understand your assets and risks in relation to the job and the assessment exercises. Get yourself in the right frame of mind and think about your likely personal impact in different exercise settings.

4 PRACTICE EXERCISES – INTERVIEWS AND PSYCHOMETRIC TESTS

Interviews and psychometric tests are regularly used as part of the assessment centre process. Often they will be delivered as a separate stage in the process but sometimes they can be included in the assessment centre so this chapter offers a quick reminder of how to do your best. It covers:

- structuring strong answers to interview questions

- your impact during an interview

- example interview questions and answers

- basic types of psychometric tests

- examples to practise on.

Interviews

Detailed guidance on how to do well in interviews is provided in other books in this series *You're Hired! Interviews* and *You're Hired! Interview Answers*, but before we look at some example questions, here is a summary of points you need to bear in mind.

Structure

If you are to be interviewed as part of an assessment centre, chances are it will be a structured, competency-based interview and it is worth exploring what this kind of interview looks like.

Typically the interviewer will ask you for an example of a situation where you have had to show the relevant behaviour and will then ask a number of follow-up questions to get at the detail of what you actually did. For example, *"Can you tell me about a time when you have had to build a new team from scratch?"*, and then followed up with:

■ *"what was the situation?"*
■ *"how did you go about it?"*
■ *"what was the outcome?"*

This is quite typical of the kind of question you can expect, so how do you go about giving a good answer?

Your best approach is to structure your answers in a way that follows the interviewer's intent. This is best summarised by the acronym **CAR** which stands for: **C**ircumstances

> **A**ction

> **R**esult.

Remembering this structure and using it to frame your answers will help the interviewer/assessor to quickly get to the attributes they are interested in. The structure also helps you to tell a more interesting and complete story, in other words give a little background to explain the situation (circumstances), then say what you actually did (action) and then say what the outcome was (result).

A well-trained interviewer, following clear interview guidelines, will follow up their initial question with a number of probe questions designed to drill down into the detail of a situation and discover what you actually did. They will be looking for evidence (both positive and negative) in relation to the competencies and the relevant behavioural indicators in the same way that they would in any other exercise that is part of the assessment centre. They are not looking for hypothetical answers or generalisations about your approach, they want to know what you did! As such, the best preparation you can do for this kind of interview is to think about relevant examples in advance.

The task, thought, people structure from Chapter 1 is helpful both as a way of preparing (try to think of examples that cover all three elements) and as a way of shaping your answers during the interview. By listening carefully to the question you can quickly tell which of these three areas the interviewer is interested in and can try to frame your answer accordingly.

Look at the following example:

"Can you tell us about a time when you had to project plan something in detail? How did you go about it?"

This is clearly a 'task' question, it is about operational delivery, the competency being explored is 'planning to achieve results', so your answer should focus on this, ideally following the CAR structure, as follows.

"I recently had to plan a design project in preparation for an exhibition: there were a number of different elements that had to be ready for the exhibition so I drew up a detailed checklist which I then turned into a project plan. I made sure that all the design elements had their own timeline as well as fitting in with the overall plan. At the same time I made sure that I built in some allowance for slippage, for example any delays in suppliers getting materials to us, then it was just a matter of regularly checking progress against the plan. I actually put the chart up on the wall so that we could all see how the various elements were coming together. In the end this paid off because we met all the deadlines and didn't have the usual last-minute panics."

The emphasis in the answer is on the implementation steps taken, ie the tasks that were performed (I considered all factors; I drew up a checklist; I turned it into a project plan; I checked regularly) so that the assessor/interviewer is quickly able to get clear evidence about your approach to planning.

Here is another answer to the same question; this time the person giving the answer has failed to identify the intent behind the question and gives a much more people-based answer.

"OK, well a recent example is the planning I had to do in advance of the Bristol exhibition. When I'm planning I like to get everyone involved so that we all know what is going on and we all understand what the key deadlines are, and this involved several meetings where we all double checked that we hadn't missed anything. This worked really well because we are a very close knit team and everyone enjoys having the chance to contribute. It also gives us the chance to be creative and we came up with lots of ideas that we would have missed if we were working independently."

In many ways this is an acceptable answer to the question but it misses the opportunity to give the assessor/interviewer clear information about your personal approach to planning and organising. This answer says more about the person's preference for collaborative and team-based working than it does about the detail of how they approach project planning. If they have time, the assessor/interviewer will have to go back and re-focus the individual so that they can get the evidence they want. If they don't have time, the individual will have missed the opportunity to give a really strong answer.

There is a difference between missing the opportunity to give a strong answer, as above, and giving an answer that is poor in the sense that it actually provides strong negative evidence in relation to the relevant competencies and performance indicators. Look at the following answer to the same question.

"Well, actually I don't tend to get involved in detailed planning. It's more a matter of making sure that we come up with the best and most creative designs. I suppose that the design brief is a sort of plan and we just make sure that we keep talking to each other about it."

An understanding assessor/interviewer might reiterate the question and give the person another chance to come up with a better answer. However, in practice, this answer makes it very easy for the assessor to tick the box that says 'poor understanding of planning processes'.

Look at the following questions and practise classifying them according to task, thought, people – it really does help you to frame your answer better.

- *"How do you go about prioritising in your current role?"*
- *"Tell me about a time when you have had to persuade someone to your point of view?"*
- *"How do you go about resource planning – can you give me an example?"*
- *"Can you give me an example of the kinds of information you use when you are making business decisions?"*
- *"Can you give me an example of a time when you have had to coach someone who was underperforming or when you needed them to change the way they were doing things?"*
- *"Can you tell me about a time when you have had to be creative and come up with a new approach to a problem?"*
- *"Tell me about your current targets? How do you monitor progress towards them?"*

The answers in order are task, people, task, thought, people, thought, and task.

Rapport

A good interviewer will be trying to put you at ease so that you can perform at your best, but the more you can help them the better. Under the time pressures of an assessment centre it is easy to forget the importance of building rapport and allowing the interview to flow easily. Answering questions in a clear and structured way (as described above) is the first step but there is more that you can do.

Ways in which you can develop rapport and make the interviewer's job easier include the following.

- Avoid being long-winded, as time is always a factor at an assessment centre, as you can see from the timetables given above. Being reasonably succinct in your answers helps the assessor to move the conversation on. It is also in your own interests to make sure that the assessor can cover all the necessary ground in terms of the competencies they need to explore.
- Concentrate and show that you are interested in the questions rather than just jumping in to a factual answer. This has the effect of making the interview feel more like a conversation between equals rather than an

inquisition! Both verbal and non-verbal behaviour can help here. Non-verbally, head nodding and leaning forwards slightly will signal your interest. Verbally, comments such as 'yes I think that's a very relevant question' or 'will an example from my time in the planning department be relevant?' show that you are cooperating with the assessor/interviewer and supporting their aim of getting good information.

■ If you lose the thread of the point you are making don't just plough on regardless, but say what is going on, for example 'I'm sorry, I've lost the thread here, can you remind me of the original question'. This helps the interviewer to 'manage' you.

■ Focus on the interview and try to avoid being distracted by everything else that is going on in the assessment centre. You should not be dwelling on the exercise you have just done or worrying about the exercises that are coming up. You need to be there 'in the moment' for the interview just as you would for any other exercise.

Be yourself

While some nervousness is inevitable, try not to let it get in the way of the assessor/interviewer getting a sense of the real 'you'. The more 'natural' you can be, the easier it will be for the interviewer/assessor to do their job.

If your research and preparation (see Chapter 3) has told you that you are particularly prone to being nervous in interviews, then it can even be worth mentioning this at the start of the interview. Don't make a big deal of it but mention that interviews make you nervous and that you will do your best to be clear and informative in the answers you give. This gives the assessor the chance to evaluate you as 'someone who gets nervous during interviews' rather than as 'someone who is just nervous and edgy in general'!

What does 'be yourself' mean in practice?

■ **Try not to put on an act that represents how you think the interviewer wants you to behave.** Unless you are a very accomplished actor this will show and it will raise doubts in the interviewer's mind about how confident they can be in your answers.

■ **Use self-disclosure.** By opening up a little and by being willing to share some information about yourself, the interviewer/assessor will find it easier to see you as someone who is open and straightforward rather than 'cagey'. Clearly you should not be pouring out your deepest personal flaws, but volunteering minor areas where you are less than perfect shows the assessor that you are trying to be honest, that you are not trying to hide anything and that you demonstrate self-awareness.

■ **Build trust.** The assessor/interviewer is doing a number of things during the interview, for example:

- they are trying to establish rapport
- they are following a structure to make sure they are covering all the required competencies
- they are looking for specific evidence
- they are assessing how confident they are in that evidence.

This last point is important: it is an aspect of how human beings evaluate each other regardless of whether it is happening at an assessment centre or not. We are continuously assessing how much we can trust what someone else is saying and an interviewer will be particularly alert to this. If the interviewer loses confidence in your honesty, you are unlikely to win back this trust in the limited time available so don't take any risks with trust! Don't pretend to have experience that you don't, don't claim knowledge that you don't have and don't exaggerate. The interviewer doesn't have to catch you out in a direct lie (not that you would do this anyway), it is enough that they lose confidence in how straightforward you are being. In the worst case it will dilute their ratings in relation to the whole interview.

The way you answer questions

How you answer questions is important, and I will cover this more fully in the example questions below. Before we get into the detail, however, here are some general points to bear in mind.

At an assessment centre, time is at a premium and your interviewer will have a very specific time slot in which to cover all the ground they need to. As a result you will usually be given quite clear guidance about the interview topics and the kind of answers from you that they will find most useful. After all, the interview is not supposed to be a game of cat and mouse; it's supposed to be an opportunity for the interviewer to explore relevant competencies, the same as any other assessment centre exercise. Anything you can do to support them in this aim is likely to serve you well and this means that a conversational but focused style of answering is what you should aim for. There are also some specific dos and don'ts that it is worth bearing in mind.

Dos and don'ts

Do

- Use your ears! Concentrate and listen to questions so that you can shape and focus your answers. For instance, if the interviewer says 'can you give me an example....?' they don't want you to ramble about your general approach to things, they want you to try and find a specific example of what you have done in the situation they are interested in.
- Look and listen for clues as to whether you are hitting the mark with your answers or whether the interviewer wants to move on. Are they trying to interject? Are they saying things like 'can you give me a *brief* example?' Being alert to this will let you judge whether the assessor is conscious of time and will help you to help them to manage the time.
- A good assessor/interviewer will give you guidance about the competency or competencies they are interested in at different points in the interview, so bear this in mind when you give your examples or answers. Are they looking for a task-based example, a people-based example, or one based on your thinking style? If you have prepared well you should be able to select examples that fit.
- Try to avoid too much technical detail or jargon in your answers unless you are specifically asked to go into this kind of detail. Your interviewer/assessor may well not be a technical expert in your area so don't assume they will know what you are talking about.

Don't

- Give long rambling answers. If you are unsure as to how much detail the interviewer wants then you can check this and adjust your style of answering accordingly. Phrases such as 'is that enough detail?' will let you assess that you are answering appropriately. This is important because under the time pressure of an assessment centre timetable your interviewer won't have the luxury of accommodating to your style of answering. If you are too long-winded they might have to settle for the answer you have given them rather than having time to probe and get the detail they need to come to a better assessment of your competence. If they want more detail, they can easily ask for it. If you hear the interviewer using phrases like 'can you say a bit more about that...?' then it gives you a clue that they want a slightly fuller answer than the one you have provided.
- Use negative examples at the expense of positive ones. The way our memories work means that it is often the negative aspects of situations that

stick in our minds. While giving examples of these will help the interviewer understand your approach to problem solving and how you persevere when faced with difficulties, too many of them will make it sound as though your life and work have been one crisis after another!

Sample interview questions and answers

It is time then to look at some example questions and answers. Remember that competency-based questions are trying to get evidence about your approach to a range of different work-based challenges. Are you methodical and systematic in your delivery style or are you a more creative implementer? How do you go about prioritising or project management? How do you track and monitor progress to ensure delivery to target, budget or quality standards? What are you like with people? How creative are you? The assessor will be trying to find links between what you say and the behavioural indicators that they are looking for. So you need to try and make their task as easy as possible.

I have already mentioned the importance of thinking through some good (ideally work-based) examples in advance of the assessment centre. It's also worth thinking about examples that are particularly relevant to task-, thought-, people-based questions. So think about times when you have had to:

■ organise something relatively complex (task)
■ deliver something to a tough deadline (task)
■ implement a new process or system (task)
■ persuade someone to your point of view (people)
■ deal with a difficult individual or group (people)
■ coach or develop someone (people)
■ make a complex decision (thought)
■ come up with a new approach or idea (thought)
■ analyse different kinds of data or information (thought).

In practice, most competency-based questions will be covered by this list.

Once you have come up with your examples, use the CAR process to frame a short description for each one, making sure that you cover the **C**ircumstances, the **A**ction you took and the **R**esult.

Example 1

Interviewer:

"Can you tell me about a time when you had to plan or re-structure something in detail?"

Poor answer:

"Yes, I was working in the Valebridge Utilities customer complaints department over the summer holiday period: we re-did the work roster because so many people were on holiday. I had a chat with all the complaints team and we agreed that something had to be done because the time to answer calls was going up and up. It had got to the point that if anyone had phoned in sick or had given in their notice we wouldn't be able to cope."

This is a task-based question, the assessor is looking for evidence of how you go about organising, and it is a poor answer because:

■ there is not enough detail about what the person actually did
■ there is no clarity about the outcome
■ the assessor/interviewer is going to have to ask a lot of follow-up questions.

Better answer:

"Yes, well, when I was working in the customer complaints department over the summer we had a staffing problem because so many people were on holiday. I took on the job of re-doing the work roster because it was clear that we were going to be understaffed if nothing was done, and the time to answer calls was going up and up. I checked the availability of all the existing staff as well as people in the stand-by pool that we could call on, matched this with the staffing requirement and then checked that this gave us enough cover. I worked out that by using four people from the stand-by pool it gave us enough hours for two shifts and this meant that the calls waiting numbers went back down to sensible levels."

This is still a succinct answer but it follows the CAR format:

■ the circumstances are covered ('we had a staffing problem')
■ the action is explained ('I re-did the work roster and checked availability')
■ the result is described ('calls waiting numbers went back down').

This makes it easy for the interviewer to tick off relevant evidence against the competency that is being explored.

An even better answer could have included a little more detail, for example who did you talk to and consult in identifying the problem, what were the targets for call answering times, what numbers of staff were involved? Anything which makes your answer richer and more convincing will help the interviewer/ assessor to get a clear 'picture' of what you did.

Example 2

Interviewer:

"Can you describe a time when you had to make a decision at work where the right choice wasn't immediately obvious?"

Poor answer:

"There was a situation in my last job where we had a choice about whether to spend a big chunk of our budget on essential maintenance or on updating our IT system. I weighed up the pros and cons for a long time before finally deciding to go for the IT spend. In the end the thing that made up my mind for me was a string of computer crashes in the same week. Not only was it really disrupting work, the complaints from staff were building up to the point that I felt I had to act."

Bearing in mind what you have learnt so far, try critiquing this answer before you read my comments below. Start by deciding if it is a task-, thought- or people-based question.

This is a thought-based question, the interviewer is interested in your judgement and how you approach decision making, for example the kind of information you use to make a choice. The answer is not a strong one because it says nothing about how you went about making the decision. All we discover from this answer is that 'I weighed up the pros and cons' and that in the end 'I had to act', but there is no description of the kind of information that was used, who was consulted or the process that was used and indeed it sounds as though in the end the decision almost made itself. This is not going to convince the assessor that you have a well thought through approach to decision making. Good responses to thought questions need to cover the nature of the decision (why it was challenging), the kind of information you had available, how you used the information and what other factors you were considering.

Better answer:
"Last year we experienced a significant budget cut which meant that I had to prioritise spending. One tricky decision that this threw up was a choice between spending budget on IT (our old system desperately needed updating) or on some much needed building refurbishment. There were some risks both ways: neglecting the refurbishment could mean that we would end up spending more money, but at the same time IT breakdowns were having a real impact on staff and customers. I had a close look at the customer complaints figures and then made an estimate of working hours lost as a result of computer downtime. It quickly became clear that the IT system was the more urgent priority, as the breakdown trend was getting worse. I laid out the figures for the senior managers, explaining the alternatives, and we agreed that the money would have to be spent on the new IT system. The new computers and software transformed the way we were working, and our customer service figures improved significantly, so I'm confident it was the right decision."

Using the CAR approach again you should be able to see why this is a much better answer.

- Circumstances: the nature of the choice is explained.
- Action: we now know what was done, what information was used and what it showed.
- Result: the outcome is described – customer service figures improved.

This answer shows that the interviewee has understood what the interviewer is looking for. On this basis the assessor/interviewer will find it much easier to identify relevant evidence.

Summary
The principles described above will apply to any competency-based interview. Always remember to:

- prepare by ensuring that you have relevant examples that you can describe
- identify what the interviewer is after (task, thought, people) and frame your answer accordingly
- use CAR to structure your answer.

Psychometric tests

It is beyond the scope of this book to give you detailed examples of all the different kinds of test you might encounter as part of an assessment centre, but there is some background information and some guiding principles that are well worth considering as a way of 'de-mystifying' these tools. (Much more information, as well as multiple examples and practice test questions relating to ability tests, can be found in another book in this series *You're Hired! Psychometric Tests*.)

Think about the assessment matrix again. In a well-designed assessment centre psychometric measures of your abilities or your personal preferences will be factored into the matrix in exactly the same way as all the other data.

For example, if you get a particularly high score on a numerical reasoning test, this is likely to be regarded as positive evidence, and hence a higher score, in relation to a competency such as 'analytical thinking'. This is because people with higher scores on ability tests such as verbal and numerical reasoning tend to be faster at using data and solving problems. In the same way, if your results on a personality or preference test suggest that you are someone who much prefers working independently rather than collaboratively, then this might lead to a lower score on a competency such as 'team leadership' but could lead to a higher score on a competency such as 'independent decision making'. As I mentioned earlier, however, the most likely place for you to have encountered tests of this kind is in advance of the assessment centre itself, as part of a screening process.

But, if you do find them built in to the assessment centre, what do you need to know?

What do psychometric tests measure?

There are two broad areas that employers are interested in when they use psychometric tests: ability and personality. There are important differences between these two categories of tests and these are illustrated in the table below.

Ability tests	Personality tests
Includes reasoning with numbers, words or diagrams	Includes personality, values and integrity questionnaires
There are absolute right and wrong answers	There is no 'correct' answer
Usually have a time limit	Are generally untimed

Ability tests

The most common types of ability test are trying to get an accurate measure of how well you can reason using numbers (numerical ability), words (verbal ability) or diagrams (abstract reasoning ability). Employers use them because they will have assessed over time that a particular level of the relevant ability is important in predicting success in whatever job is under consideration. They help the employer to predict capabilities such as:

■ how quickly and accurately you can reach conclusions based on complex information
■ how good you are at reading through complex information and extracting what is relevant
■ how good you are at understanding and using numbers to inform your decision making.

There are large numbers of ability tests on the market and it is not possible to illustrate them all here. What they have in common is that they are comparing your scores with a relevant comparison group (for example graduates or middle managers) so as to assess whether you are above or below the 'average' in terms of the specific ability that is being measured.

Just to give you a flavour of how these tests are most commonly presented (whether in paper and pencil format or on-line computer presentation) here are some illustrations covering numerical and verbal reasoning.

Numerical reasoning tests

In using numerical reasoning tests employers are not interested in your mathematical ability; they are interested in whether you can make sense of and use the kinds of numbers that come up in business. As such they are not testing your ability to do algebra or solve equations. What they are looking at is your ability to use basic arithmetic techniques (including percentages and ratios) to answer straightforward work-based questions. In practice this means:

- identifying relevant facts from tables provided
- working out percentages
- working out averages
- using basic ratios, decimals and fractions.

Your mindset and your confidence is a big factor in doing well in this kind of test. Many people develop a mental block about numerical information and the best preparation you can do is to practise.

IMPROVING YOUR SCORES

I recently worked with someone who typically got rather poor scores on numerical reasoning tests. A big factor in this was nervousness and a tendency to panic when faced with a problem that he couldn't solve. Practice and confidence building, together with some basic test-taking technique, enabled him to more than double his previous scores.

Make sure that you can work out percentages and practise extracting information from tables; research shows that practice has a big impact on scores. Practice will also help you to become familiar with the kind of language used in the tests. Some tests; will deliberately use business terminology in the questions and this can be off-putting if you do not use this kind of language day to day: terms such as 'capital ratios', 'partner equity', 'sales revenue', 'profit margin'. Don't be fazed by this terminology, it is usually easy to work out what the question is getting at without having to have an accountant's understanding of specific business terms.

Practice and familiarity are particularly important in the context of an assessment centre given that your head will be full of other activities and distractions.

The most regularly used tests will present you with questions in one of two styles: table-based questions or 'standalone' questions.

Table-based questions will follow the format of giving you data in the form of tables (or sometimes graphs) followed by a number of different questions which you can only answer by referring to the tables. You will usually be asked a number of questions based on the same set of information so it is well worth taking a minute to familiarise yourself with this information at the start of the test.

'Standalone' questions contain all the information you need in the question itself – you don't have to refer to any other source of information. You may be familiar with this kind of question from school, the main difference being that they will usually be presented in a business context and use business terminology. The computations you need to do are usually quite straightforward and the secret with this kind of question is usually checking the information to see what 'sums' you are being asked to do.

Example: Table-based format

Valebridge Adult Education Centre room occupancy figures 2011

Type of room	Number of rooms available	Average number of days each room occupied
Small seminar rooms (up to 8 people)	10	135
Large seminar rooms (up to 12 people)	7	180
Small conference rooms (up to 20 people)	8	98
Large conference rooms (up to 50 people)	4	64
Garden room (up to 80 people)	1	75

1. **In 2011, how many days in the year was each large seminar room occupied on average?**

   A – 300   B – 85   C – 390   D – 180   E – 135

   Answer: 180 – you don't need to do any computation, it's just a matter of finding the right number in column 2.

2. **How many rooms in total are available in the education centre?**

   A – 48   B – 30   C – 27   D – 36   E – 64

   Answer: 30 – simply a matter of adding all the numbers in column 1.

3. **If every small seminar room was full and every small conference room was full on a particular day, how many people would this be in total?**

   A – 320   B – 200   C – 240   D – 270   E – Can't say

Answer: 240 – the number of people in small seminar rooms is
80 (10 x 8); the number of people in small conference rooms is 160
(20 x 8); add the two together to get 240.

4. **Assuming that rooms are available on 220 days of the year, what
   percentage of the available time, on average, are the large seminar rooms
   occupied? (To the nearest whole number)**

   A – 82%   B – 75%   C – 65%   D – 25%   E – Can't say

   Answer: 82% – simply 180 as a percentage of 220 (81.81%) rounded to
   the nearest whole number.

Example: Specific question-based format

1. **At Valebridge Electrical Components, in an average week the production line is
   down for 5.5 hours for essential maintenance. Lost production, per hour when
   the line is down, is 1100 units. How many units are lost in an average week?**

   A – 3,800   B – 6,050   C – 4,000   D – 2,400   E – 24,000

   Answer: hopefully you will have worked out that it is 5.5 x 1,100 = 6,050.

2. **If the production line was only down for 5.0 hours, how many additional
   units would be produced in an average week?**

   A – 50   B – 250   C – 550   D – 750   E – 150

   Answer: you are told that lost production per hour is 1100; this equates
   to lost production of 550 in half an hour. Since you have gained half an
   hour's production the answer is 550.

3. **Every unit of lost production has a potential value of £0.45. What would be
   the value of lost production if the line was down for eight hours?**

   A – £3,960   B – £6,050   C – £2,220   D – £3,500   E – £1,500

   Answer: £3,960 – you know that one hour of lost production costs 1100
   units so 8 hours of lost production will cost 1,100 x 8 = 8,800. Multiply
   this by 0.45 to get the value in pounds.

The skills needed for these two question formats are broadly the same; the
main difference being that in the table-based formats you have to first identify
the relevant information before you can calculate your answer.

A lot of numerical tests allow you to use calculators if you wish and these will often be provided. If you are told that calculators are permitted then it is better to use your own (one that you are familiar with) rather than having to get to know a new instrument in 'real time' during the test! Our advice, unless you are used to using complex calculators, is to choose a simple machine with large buttons and to practise using it in advance, particularly how to work out percentages.

TOP TIPS FOR NUMERICAL TESTS

■ Practise using numerical information: for example, increase your familiarity with extracting information from tables. For table-based questions, give a minute to familiarising yourself with the information they contain.

■ Make sure you can work out percentages and brush up on your long division and long multiplication. Get to know and trust your calculator.

■ Read the questions carefully, don't do calculations that you don't have to! Sometimes the answer can simply be read from the table.

■ Make full use of the practice items you will be given at the start of any test. Make sure you understand the format.

■ Don't be put off by business language and terminology. If you are not familiar with business language then make time during your preparation to look up specific words or read business-related material.

■ If you are going to guess, guess wisely, for example is the answer going to be in 'tens' or in 'thousands'.

Verbal reasoning tests

Employers use verbal reasoning tests because they want to see how well you can apply logic and reach the right conclusion based on the kind of information that you read. How we reason and solve problems is a huge area of study in itself but typically these tests are trying to assess the following:

■ **your verbal comprehension:** can you look at a passage of information and find the right information within it?
■ **your ability to apply logic:** can you make a sensible judgement based on the information you are given?

■ **your vocabulary:** do you understand what words and sentences mean; are you able to find alternative words or alternative ways of expressing an idea?

The verbal tests you encounter will typically follow a format where you are asked to read a passage of information and then answer a number of multiple choice questions based on the information contained in the passage. The correct answers are given in bold in each case. If you are unsure about why any of these answers is correct then you should seek out more practice items, for example in *You're Hired! Psychometric Tests*.

Most verbal tests will warn you to base your answers on the information given and not on your own knowledge or opinions about the subject matter of the passage. So, base your answers only on the information you are given even if you have a contrary view!

Example: Verbal reasoning

Read the following passage and then answer the questions:

The science of Genetics has developed significantly over the last 60 years, starting with the explanation of the 'double helix' by Watson and Crick in the 1950s and reaching the point where we now have a map of the whole human genome. It is hard to overestimate the impact and importance of this area of scientific endeavour; it has started to, and will continue to, impact every aspect of our lives. This has already started to raise ethical and moral questions that we did not have to trouble ourselves with, except hypothetically, until relatively recently. While in the past our moral philosophers might have agonised theoretically over issues such as free will, biological determinism and animal rights, we are now faced with these as real moral dilemmas because of what genetics has taught us. The extent to which our behaviour is biologically determined, the degree to which our abilities and predispositions are inherited, and the smallness of the gap between our genetic makeup and that of our primate cousins are now real rather than theoretical challenges. The challenge to business is also imminent – how long will it be before genetic screening determines the size of our insurance payments and before employers use genetic testing rather than interviews to determine our character and suitability for a given job?

Comprehension questions

1. Which of the following topics is not specifically mentioned in the passage?

    a. Human genome

    b. Animal rights

    c. Genetic screening

    d. Fertility treatment

    e. The double helix

2. Which one of these statements most accurately reflects the key points of the passage?

    a. There are significant dangers in continuing to advance our knowledge of genetics

    b. Watson and Crick were important figures in establishing the importance of genetic science

    c. Genetic screening will become increasingly important

    d. Advances in genetics will raise a number of ethical and practical challenges

    e. Moral philosophy has become outdated

3. Which of the following issues are specifically mentioned as ones that moral philosophers used to worry about?

    a. Genetic screening, human rights, moral questions

    b. Business challenges, genetic testing, ethics

    c. Free will, biological determinism, animal rights

    d. Hypothetical questions, character, genetic tests

    e. Genetics, primate rights, employment law

The answers are: 1 – d   2 – d   3 – c

Logic questions

Based on the information in the passage, are the following statements true, false or can't say?

4. 'Genetics has started to impact every aspect of our lives'

    a. True   b. False   c. Can't say

5. 'Watson did most of the important work on the double helix'

    a. True   b. False   c. Can't say

6. 'The study of genetics has not revealed much that is new in the last 60 years'

    a. True   b. False   c. Can't say

The answers are: 4 – a   5 – c   6 – b

Vocabulary questions

7. Which of the following words would best replace the word 'dilemmas' in line ten of the passage?

    a. problems
    b. choices
    c. difficulties
    d. responsibilities
    e. opportunities

8. Which of the following words would best replace the word 'agonised' in line nine of the passage?

    a. worried
    b. painful
    c. considered
    d. pondered
    e. discussed

9. Which of the following words is closest to having the opposite meaning to the word 'imminent' in line 15 of the passage?

    a. pending
    b. distant
    c. confused
    d. actual
    e. theoretical

The answers are: 7 – b   8 – a   9 – b

TOP TIPS FOR VERBAL TESTS

There are a number of reasons why you might get a score lower than you deserve when completing tests of this kind. These include lack of familiarity with the test format, nervousness, and poor preparation. Avoid these pitfalls by:

- practising – make sure you understand the logic of the question
- recognising when you are stuck and you are better served by moving on to the next item
- reading questions very carefully to make sure you understand what is being asked of you – you can waste a lot of time otherwise
- developing your own sense of which kinds of item you find easy or hard and using this to focus your practice.

Above all – don't panic!

Preference tests

Preference tests are measures of your preferred or habitual ways of behaving or responding to different situations – in other words the way of behaving that is most typical of you. The most common type of preference test is a personality questionnaire. The idea behind these tests is that we are all reasonably consistent in our behaviour and this is because our behaviours are shaped, in part, by our personality. Look at the following questions and think about your own personal style.

- Do you tend to be organised and systematic or are you more easy-going about plans or deadlines?
- Would people describe you as being calm and collected or as someone who is more emotional and passionate?
- Do you like to have lots of people around you or are you someone who prefers a good deal of privacy?

Of course we all do different things on different occasions, but our behaviour is not random. Our personality is made up of all the preferences that shape our behaviour in one direction, and move us away from another direction. Employers are interested in measuring your personality because it provides them with information about your personal style: the sorts of tasks and activities that you naturally enjoy and those situations that you may wish to avoid.

There are lots of different ways of measuring your personal preferences and a variety of headings that test constructors use to summarise your personality. One of the most widely used structures is illustrated below.

Personality domain	Example questions	Yes	No
Openness to experience	I prefer to have variety in my day		
	I enjoy hearing new ideas		
	I have a vivid imagination		
Conscientiousness	I like working towards a plan		
	I always keep my promises		
	I pay attention to the details		
Extraversion	I want to be the centre of attention		
	I like having lots to do		
	I enjoy being around other people		
Agreeableness	I believe that other people are trustworthy		
	I try to avoid getting into disagreements		
	I feel sorry for people less fortunate than me		
Emotional stability	I rarely worry about things		
	I find it easy to get over setbacks		
	It takes a lot to make me feel angry		

The most common tests will show you statements such as the ones above and then ask how much you agree or disagree with each statement. In this way the test builds up a profile of you, highlighting any strong preferences that you have.

Dos and don'ts for preference tests

The key thing to remember about preference/personality tests is that there are no right or wrong answers! Trying to manipulate your answers so as to give the answers that you think they want is always a mistake for the following reasons.

■ There is a big risk that you will misinterpret what they are looking for.
■ Most personality tests have consistency and honesty scales built into them that will reveal if you are trying to present yourself in the best light. Attempts to manipulate the test will always arouse suspicion in the person interpreting it.
■ Pretending to be someone you are not will show up in the other exercises that you complete as part of the assessment centre and will lead to an

inconsistent set of scores in the assessment matrix – again arousing suspicion.
- It does not make much sense to 'fake' a set of preferences in order to get a job that you will then hate!

The simple answer then, is to respond to preference/personality tests as honestly and straightforwardly as you can.

IN A NUTSHELL

- Interviews and psychometric tests, if they are used as part of an assessment centre, will provide information that will be used in the same way as information from any other exercise – in other words to get a fully rounded picture of your capabilities.
- For interviews, prepare by thinking through examples of relevant experience and practise describing them succinctly. Use the CAR approach to frame your answers.
- There are two main types of psychometric tests – ability tests and preference tests. Ability tests have right or wrong answers, while preference tests do not and are aiming to get at the 'real you'.
- Psychometric tests work by comparing your responses to those of other, similar people.
- For preference tests employers most commonly use the scores to profile you against relevant competencies.
- Your confidence in taking ability tests will be greatly improved by practice, so make use of test publishers' websites and any other practice examples you can find in relevant books.
- The best policy with preference tests is to be honest and be yourself!

5 PRACTICE EXERCISES – ROLE PLAYS

This chapter will give you a number of tips for performing well during role play exercises as well as giving you examples of role play briefs. Most importantly it will help you to see the exercise from the role players' and the assessors' point of view so that you can perform at your best. It will include:

■ outlines of the different types of role play

■ tips for performing well

■ full examples of role play briefs and how they work in practice.

Getting ready for role play

As we saw in Chapter 2, role plays are very commonly used in assessment centres as a way of observing and evaluating your competence, particularly in dealing with different interpersonal situations.

To recap, the most typical role play simulations you will encounter include:

- a meeting with an unhappy customer or member of the public to deal with a complaint or issue
- a meeting with an unhappy member of staff
- a fact–finding meeting to explore someone else's view of an issue or gather relevant information from them
- a business development or sales-based meeting
- a meeting where you have to influence someone more senior than you in the organisation
- a meeting where you have to negotiate or bargain to get to the best possible outcome.

In a well-designed assessment centre, the role player will be a professional actor who has a very clear brief to follow – both in terms of the character they are playing and the situation. You will be given a brief explaining the

---

ACT NATURALLY

A lot of people tell us that 'they are no good at role plays' and that they find it hard to deal with the artificiality of the situation. If you are the kind of person who is particularly daunted by the need to 'act' in this situation, then your preparation is key to your success. Use the following examples to imagine yourself into the situation and think what it will take for you to behave as naturally as possible. You might want to share some of these situations with a friend or colleague and practise having the conversation. Don't let yourself use the 'I'm no good at role playing' argument as an excuse. It won't impress assessors who will often be evaluating you in terms of how well you can adjust your behaviour to meet the needs of different situations. By saying 'I'm no good at role playing' you are effectively admitting that this is something you can't do!

---

situation, typically some time to prepare and then will be asked to conduct the meeting.

The examples that follow all contain the participant's brief and, this is the part you usually wouldn't get to see, the actor's brief, so that you get some insight to the character they are playing. Also included are some dos and don'ts about how to handle that kind of situation, and some guidance on how behaviours are likely to map on to particular competencies.

Example role play 1 – the unhappy customer

Participant's brief

Scenario: you are taking the role of a new manager at Cowbridge Car Imports (CCI), it is your first week in the new job and you do not have any previous experience in this particular business. One of your colleagues, Alex Hilton, has been taken ill and at very short notice you have been asked to pick up his workload. Your boss is Chris Barber, the head of operations, and she recognises that you are being thrown in at the deep end but hopes that you will be able to apply your general experience to tackling the various issues that are likely to arise.

The meeting will start in 30 minutes.

Email: *Sorry to dump this on you at such short notice but a problem has come up with the Primrose Garage Group. They buy about 150 cars a year from us and their purchasing manager (Lennie Duff) had a meeting in the diary for today with Alex. I wonder if you can pick it up. I really don't want us to cancel the meeting because, as you will see from the attached note, it looks as though they are unhappy. Alex mentioned something to me last week about us needing to treat them carefully because there is a risk that they will start importing their vehicles directly rather than using us! Personally I don't think this is a big risk because I think they will struggle to get a better deal anywhere else.*

It's probably worth you knowing that the restructure of the delivery department has probably had an impact on this complaint (we have had to replace the delivery manager); but I'm pretty confident that the new person we have put in place, Sam Khan, will turn it around quickly, as he is very experienced.

See if you can find out what the problem is. I have warned Lennie that you will be at the meeting rather than Alex.

Many thanks

Chris

Attached email: Hi Alex, I'm glad that we have a meeting scheduled because there are a couple of things I would like to raise. The first is that I'm sorry to report that I'm still having a problem with your delivery department. The three cars we took delivery of last week had not been properly prepared, there was protective plastic still on the door sills and protective wax still on the wheel trims, and all three cars were late! This caused us significant extra work in getting the cars ready for customer handover.

I know that we have had a very good service from you in the past but this is now the third time this has happened in the last month. What's going on in your delivery department? I value the business relationship we have had for the last three years but if we don't get customer ready cars from you then we might as well start importing the vehicles ourselves.

Sorry to sound so negative but this has given me a big headache over the last couple of weeks. Look forward to meeting later.

Cheers

Lennie

This scenario is quite typical of the kind of briefing you will get for a role play exercise: it gives you enough information to start a meeting but does not go into any detail. Before reading on, think through the general approach you might take to a meeting of this kind. What kind of objectives might you set yourself before the meeting? What would a good outcome look like? Put yourself in Lennie's shoes, what is he likely to be thinking or expecting from the meeting?

Now, here is the bit you don't normally get to see – the exercise from the actor's point of view:

Actor's brief

Scenario: *you are playing the part of Lennie Duff, the purchasing manager of the Primrose Garage Group. The group owns 17 garages in the south of England and is an independent seller of new and used cars. One of your strongest business lines is the supply of specialist and more unusual vehicles – often imported. Your biggest supplier of imported cars is Cowbridge Car Imports (CCI) and you have recently had a problem with the standard of service you have been getting from them. CCI have given you a very good service over the last three years, and their pricing is competitive, but poor service over the last month has caused you a significant problem. Cars have been delivered late and they have been poorly prepared – in other words your people have had to do extra work in terms of cleaning and finishing the cars before they could be passed on to customers. In one case a customer was kept waiting for an hour while your team frantically got the car ready!*

You want a strong reassurance that this problem won't happen again and are willing to negotiate quite hard to get this reassurance. Your ultimate threat is to take your business away from CCI, but you really don't want to do this since it would take time to set up your own import service or to find another supplier that is as good as CCI. Your other option is to try and get CCI to agree to a penalty payment for any car that is late or badly prepared. You have a figure of about £500 per car in mind. Your main concern, however, is that you start getting a better service, because your reputation with your customers is at stake!

Your personality: *you are straight talking and very matter of fact in your style – not rude but not particularly interested in small talk. You don't like waffle and will want to hear that practical steps are going to be taken to solve the problem. You don't expect miracles but you do want some clear reassurance. Customer service is very important to you personally as well as from a business point of view. At the start of the meeting you are irritated rather than angry. Things that will placate you are:*

- *an apology*
- *an explanation*

- *the participant taking responsibility rather than passing the buck*
- *ideas about how the situation will be improved*
- *showing an interest in you, your business and the problem*
- *willingness to start building a relationship with you.*

Things that will annoy you are:

- *defensiveness*
- *an unwillingness to take any responsibility, e.g. 'I'm new here so I can't do anything'*
- *a refusal to acknowledge the problem or offer an apology.*

What this should make clear is that **they will respond to you depending on how you treat them**. A common misperception of role play exercises is that the actor is briefed to behave in a particular way, for example to be awkward, throughout the exercise. In fact, most good role play actors will be continuously modifying their performance based on what you say and how you say it – just as the real person would. This also means that you need to be attentive to the person you are talking to, continuously monitoring how they are reacting to what you say – just like you would in a real life conversation. So, be yourself and let the actor do the acting!

You will also have noticed that there is a potential negotiating point built in to this scenario, namely the prospect of compensation for any cars that are delivered late. Don't be tempted to get into a win-lose conversation about this. Unless the exercise is specifically designed as a negotiation task (and this one isn't) getting too hung up on arguing about numbers is usually unhelpful. It is better to try and deal with the underlying issues rather than dig your heels in over a specific number. If you find that the person is being particularly dogmatic about this point then think about what will help to move the conversation on. Take a look at the following suggestions:

- Concede that the point is worth considering but that you would like some more time to think about it because it is important to get it right.
- Say that you understand where the person is coming from but that you would like to talk about it later after the problem has been fixed.
- Suggest that you are happy to talk about compensation but that you would like to consult your colleagues first.

What you should avoid doing is:

- Dogmatically refusing to consider compensation: this will just annoy the role player (in character) and risk leaving the assessors with the view that you are reading the situation badly or that you are inflexible.
- Caving in to the request without giving it due consideration: this risks leaving the role player with the feeling that you would find it easier to pay compensation than actually fix the problem and risks the assessors feeling that you lack the confidence to stand your ground.

A good sequence to consider in conducting the meeting is the following:

- Introduce yourself, say who you are and why you are attending the meeting, make it clear that you are keen to try and help in resolving the problem.
- Try to establish some rapport but don't try and push small talk if the actor is clearly keen to get down to business.
- Acknowledge the problem and, if appropriate, apologise. In the case of this scenario CCI is clearly at fault so recognise this and don't try to be defensive.
- Show that you recognise Lennie's point of view, say 'that must have put you in a difficult position with your staff/your customer'.
- Ask questions, show some curiosity about the business and the individual – this helps to build the relationship.
- Be willing to share some information about yourself: you are new to the business, what has your first week been like, what are you enjoying, etc.
- Make a proposal: explain what you and the business are going to do to make sure that the problem won't happen again. Explain that the problem has been picked up internally and that steps have already been taken by appointing a new delivery manager.
- Take personal responsibility by saying what **you** are going to do, establish a line of communication, say that you want Lennie to call you personally if there is a problem.
- Close the meeting by making it clear what is going to happen next, offer some clear next steps. In this scenario a good proposal would be to suggest a meeting between you, Sam Khan and Lennie so that you can introduce Sam to an important customer and establish some clear service levels – this shows you are being proactive and shows your concern with customer service.

Dos and don'ts

Do

■ Take the exercise seriously, don't be flippant as this will annoy the character you are meeting and won't go down well with the assessor.

■ Put yourself in the shoes of the person you are meeting – not the actor… the person!

■ Try to imagine yourself in the real situation and not in a role play – this will help you to be yourself.

■ Think about the exercise as a whole, consider the task, thought, people aspects to the situation.

Don't

■ Try to second guess the exercise or the role player: for example you can tie yourself in knots by basing your behaviour on what you think the role player might know or what they don't know, so treat the situation as real!

■ Dogmatically stick to a pre-prepared agenda, respond to the person in real time and be willing to adjust your approach accordingly.

■ Panic if the conversation seems to be getting 'sticky'! The role player is not briefed to be unreasonable but at the same time they are trying to provide a challenge for you. If you do seem to be stuck, stay in character but try saying something like 'Look Lennie, this conversation isn't going the way I hoped, what can I do to satisfy you that the situation is going to be resolved?'

Relationship to competencies

Different organisations and different assessment centre designers will attach different competencies to exercises in accordance with the assessment matrix for that particular assessment centre. For all the examples in this book, however, I will illustrate the relationship to competencies by selecting two competencies, and the relevant behavioural indicators, that are typical of that particular exercise. The idea is to give you a sense of the kinds of behaviours that the assessors are likely to be looking for in a particular exercise.

Competency	Indicators for this exercise
Achievement orientated	• Takes decisions, does not put everything off • Suggests clear actions to solve the problem • Positive and optimistic about the chances of success • Is not fazed by the challenges Lennie raises • Summarises and agrees clear next steps at the end of the exercises
Influencing and persuading	• Establishes rapport with Lennie, introduces self clearly, asks questions to understand Lennie's background • Listens well, acknowledges Lennie's point of view • Deals with the issue of compensation confidently but politely • Starts to build a relationship with Lennie, suggests regular meetings and follow up

Example role play 2 – the unhappy member of staff

Participant's brief

Scenario: you are taking the role of a new manager at Cowbridge Car Imports (CCI), it is your first week in the new job and you do not have any previous experience in this particular business. One of your colleagues, Alex Hilton, has been taken ill and at very short notice you have been asked to pick up his workload. Your boss is Chris Barber, the head of operations, and she recognises that you are being thrown in at the deep end but hopes that you will be able to apply your general experience to tackling the various issues that are likely to arise.

The meeting will start in 30 minutes.

Email: *Sorry to drop you in at the deep end like this but we have a problem with one of Alex's team and I wonder if you can help. Alex was scheduled to have a meeting with Frankie James today and from the messages I have received it sounds like a fairly urgent issue. I gather that it was Frankie who asked for the meeting. I really don't want to cancel the meeting but I have to be in Birmingham this afternoon so can you pick it up?*

I met Frankie in the warehouse yesterday and he clearly wasn't happy. Let me give you a bit of background.

Frankie is 35 and has been with us for seven years as warehouse supervisor, he reports directly to Alex and as far as I know they have a pretty good relationship but when I met Frankie yesterday he started asking me if I was OK with writing him a reference for some other job he was applying for! Frankie is a really solid performer, he keeps the warehouse crew on their toes, and they are not the easiest bunch of people to manage. I really don't want to lose him, especially if our growth plans over the next three years go ahead – a good warehouse operation will be essential. I asked him what it was that was making him look for a job elsewhere but he just muttered something about needing a change. I don't know what conversations he has had with Alex but I'd really like you to try and get to the bottom of the issue. It could be that someone 'neutral' will be able to get him to open up a bit. I don't think it's about money because he had a good pay rise three months ago. I'd be really grateful for anything you can do.

Many thanks

Chris

PS I've explained to Frankie that you will be handling the meeting for Alex.

Once again, this is a typical scenario, not much in the way of detailed information and this in itself should give you the clue that you will need to do a lot of exploring during the meeting.

As before, think through the general approach you might take to a meeting of this kind before you read the actor's brief. What kind of objectives might you set yourself before the meeting? What would a good outcome look like? Put yourself in Frankie's shoes, what is he likely to be thinking or expecting from the meeting?

Actor's brief

Scenario: you are playing the part of Frankie James, the warehouse supervisor at Cowbridge Car Imports. The group owns 17 garages in the south of England and is an independent seller of new and used cars. One of your strongest business lines is the supply of specialist and more unusual vehicles – often imported. You are responsible for supervising the teams who look after three large warehouses where cars are stored before they are dispatched to customers. At peak times you can be storing anything up to 100 cars with 20 to 30 cars coming in and out on a typical day. In all you have about

15 people reporting to you and you pride yourself in the strong relationship you have with the warehouse staff. They can be an awkward lot and your approach is to be very fair and honest in the way that you deal with them. This has gained you a lot of respect and you take a lot of pride in running a very smooth operation.

In recent months you have raised with Alex the possibility of being given the title of supply manager to reflect the fact that your responsibilities have grown a lot over the last two years, for example commissioning and taking on a new warehouse as well as the two you were previously looking after. In reality you are more interested in some new challenges, not just the title. Alex did not seem particularly keen, especially when you suggested that you would like the business to pay for you to attend a one-month management training course at a local college. The way you look at it is that you have learned how to manage through practical experience but that if you want your career to progress it's time that you had some formal training to back this up. After all it is the business that will benefit. You have asked three times for another meeting with Alex to talk it over but he has put you off every time and you are starting to get very frustrated. Because you are quite reserved it is not easy for you to push your own agenda like this, which just adds to your frustration. You love your job but it is getting to the point that you feel undervalued and if you can't see any prospect of advancement within CCI then perhaps it's time that you moved on.

You have now been told that a new manager has been asked to meet with you because Alex is ill. You are prepared to listen to what this person has to say but you are really looking for some reassurance that you have prospects in CCI.

Your personality: you are a straightforward but quite reserved individual, not prone to talking about your feelings and not really comfortable in singing your own praises – you expect people to recognise the good work you do without you having to make a fuss about it. You give 100% to your job and you expect the business to show the same loyalty and commitment to you. You need some variety and change in your work to keep you motivated and this has been missing for the last six months, everything is pretty well bedded in and running smoothly; you're not feeling particularly challenged at the moment. You are interested to meet the new manager but a little unsure about how they will be able to help. Your first reaction to questions is likely to be 'everything is fine'. At the start of the meeting you are a little reserved but friendly and quite happy to open up if the person builds some rapport with you, shows some interest and sounds like they are keen to help. Things that will help you to open up are:

- *the participant showing interest in you as a person*
- *the participant sharing information about themselves*
- *the participant making it clear that the business really values you*
- *the participant showing interest by offering personal support*
- *the participant asking open questions to better understand your situation*
- *willingness to start building a relationship with you*
- *specific suggestions, e.g. talking to Alex or to Chris on Frankie's behalf.*

Things that will make you keep your distance or even get cagey are:

- *a professional front that stops you getting to know each other*
- *an unwillingness to take any responsibility, e.g. 'I'm new here so I can't do anything'*
- *any sense that they are hiding things from you, e.g. not mentioning expansion plans*
- *any lack of openness, e.g. not mentioning that Chris is worried*
- *any lack of commitment to doing something about the situation.*

Once again you can see the exercise from the role player's point of view: there are no tricks or traps, their performance will be based on how you handle them. In this kind of role play, your willingness to explore, ask questions and show that you are committed to a good outcome are key to you doing well.

A good sequence to consider in conducting the meeting is as follows:

- Introduce yourself, say who you are and why you are attending the meeting, make it clear that you are there to listen and are keen to try and help in resolving the problem.
- Try to establish rapport and share information about yourself as a way of building trust.
- Show that you recognise Frankie's point of view, say 'I can see why you have been getting frustrated'.
- Ask questions, show curiosity about Frankie's aspirations, motivations and ambitions.
- Take personal responsibility by saying what **you** are going to do, if appropriate say you will speak with Alex and/or Chris.

Dos and don'ts

Do

- Take the exercise seriously. Set yourself the objective of Frankie feeling better when he leaves the room than when he walked in.
- Put yourself in the shoes of the person you are meeting – not the actor... the person! How would you feel in Frankie's situation?
- Think about the exercise as a whole, consider the task, thought, people aspects to the situation.

Don't

- Jump to conclusions about Frankie. Give yourself time to explore before you start offering solutions.
- Merely act as a go-between. Show through your words that you are personally interested in keeping Frankie.
- Allow the conversation to stay at a superficial level. Be willing to explore some of the potentially contentious areas.

Relationship to competencies

Once again, here are some typical competencies, together with the behavioural indicators, that assessors would be likely to be looking for in this exercise.

Competency	Indicators for this exercise
Achievement orientated	• Takes decisions, does not put everything off • Suggests clear actions to solve the problem • Positive and optimistic about Frankie's future prospects • Summarises and agrees clear next steps at the end of the exercises • Does not over-promise or make unrealistic commitments
Influencing and persuading	• Establishes rapport with Frankie, introduces self clearly, asks questions to understand Frankie's point of view • Listens well, acknowledges Frankie's point of view • Uses self-disclosure as a way of building trust • Starts to build a relationship with Frankie, suggests regular meetings and follow up
Motivating others	• Recognises Frankie's desire for progression, agrees to support it • Emphasises the value CCI places on Frankie's contribution • Paints a picture of a positive future • Explores Frankie's motivations and needs, does not assume

Example role play 3 – influencing upwards

Participant's brief

Scenario: you are taking the role of a new manager at Cowbridge Car Imports (CCI), it is your first week in the new job and you do not have any previous experience in this particular business. One of your colleagues, Alex Hilton, has been taken ill and at very short notice you have been asked to pick up his workload. Your boss is Chris Barber, the head of operations, and she recognises that you are being thrown in at the deep end but hopes that you will be able to apply your general experience to tackling the various issues that are likely to arise.

The meeting will start in 30 minutes.

Email from Alex Hilton: *I understand that you have a meeting coming up with Chris; this is a matter I planned to raise but I would be very grateful if you could discuss the following while I am away. I think Chris knows the general background but I'm a bit worried that she doesn't understand the urgency, the last time I raised it she was very offhand.*

In the last couple of weeks I've been going over some contracts that are up for renewal in the next three months, just to check if there was anything we needed to re-negotiate, and I have found a potential problem.

We have been supplying vehicles to Vale Fleet Contracts (VFC) for three years now at a fixed price that we agreed in 2008. They have written to me and it looks like they are assuming that this contract will continue on the same terms. I don't think we can let this happen. I know that they are a very significant customer but if we apply the same prices, we will effectively be making a loss of £300 per vehicle by the end of the financial year. If you multiply this by the 190 vehicles that we will be supplying over that period then you can see why the contract has to be renegotiated!

Not even VFC can be expecting us to maintain prices over four years!

There has been some history with VFC, the original contract was negotiated by Chris and VFC drove a very hard bargain. At the time we desperately needed the volume and in reality I think Chris gave them too good a deal, and we are going to pay a price for it if we can't renegotiate. I have been trying to raise the issue with Jenny Mills, their contracts manager, but she says it's nothing to do with her because this contract was agreed 'at high level' by one of the directors and that she can't get involved.

I really do think that Chris needs to handle this, she has the personal relationship with the director concerned (I think his name is Anderson) and I think the meeting needs to happen quickly. If we don't get back to them this week they will start to assume that the contract is OK and that will make any negotiation even worse.

I'm not sure if there is something I'm missing here, to me it's a no brainer, we have to have a new contract on better terms and quickly.

See what you can do to talk Chris round, it may land better coming from someone impartial!

Best of luck

Alex

So, here we have a situation where you need to raise an issue with your boss and persuade them to take some action. Once again, think through the general approach you might take to a meeting of this kind before you read the actor's brief. What kind of objectives might you set yourself before the meeting? What objections do you anticipate? What would a good outcome look like? Put yourself in Chris's shoes, why might she be reluctant to she the meeting with VFC?

Actor's brief

Scenario: you are playing the part of Chris Barber, the director of operations at Cowbridge Car Imports. The group owns 17 garages in the south of England and is an independent seller of new and used cars. One of your strongest business lines is the supply of specialist and more unusual vehicles, often imported. You are responsible for all operational matters and this includes large contracts with key customers.

One of these is VFC, your second biggest customer. You are aware that the contract with them is up for renewal; you negotiated the original deal, a deal that you felt was OK at the time because of the sheer number of vehicles they were buying – nearly 400 cars a year. You knew at the time that the profit margin on the contract was very tight but you are unaware that your increasing costs in the meantime now make this contract unprofitable.

VFC drove a very hard bargain. Nigel Anderson, their sales director was almost intimidating at the contract meetings and you found him very difficult to negotiate with. Therefore you are not looking forward to having to go into another round of meetings with him. As far as you are concerned, it would be much better for the contract to be handled by Alex and their contracts manager without having to involve you. You are slightly guilty that you have been putting this matter off.

Your personality: you are a very sales-orientated director, always very busy and a bit disorganised. While very capable in your job, you are prone to taking on too many things and leaving things to the last minute. You have never been very good at delegation and in recent months you have been trying hard to pass things to your team rather than do everything yourself.

You are a highly optimistic individual, tending to assume that everything will turn out well, and can become frustrated by people who just come to you with problems rather than solutions. In relation to this particular contract issue, you really do not want to get involved unless the participant can persuade you of the importance of the matter.

At the start of the meeting you will be friendly, ask how the new manager is settling in, and be keen to keep the small talk going rather than get down to the issue. If the participant is persistent then you will start to engage about the contract but will still be trying to pass the buck. If the participant starts to make good clear arguments about the importance of the contract then you will reluctantly agree to take it forward but will be vague about when you will have the meeting. The participant should be trying to get you to commit to taking action urgently: you will be willing to do this only if they are persuasive and reasonably tenacious in nailing you down. Deep down you know that you will have to get involved so you are wiling to be persuaded but only very reluctantly.

Things that will get you to commit to action are:

- a very clear explanation of the issues
- a supportive and polite approach, trying to win you over rather than preach at you

- *the participant appealing to your judgement rather than just trying to browbeat you*
- *the participant exploring the background with you and giving you credit for pulling off a major contract in the first place*
- *the participant showing interest by offering personal support*
- *the participant showing patience and tenacity in bringing you back to the main point of the discussion.*

Things that will make you prevaricate or start to irritate you are:

- *any caginess or lack of clarity in presenting the problem*
- *anything which sounds disrespectful or hectoring*
- *anything which sounds too deferential or undersells the importance of the issue*
- *lack of clarity about what you need to do.*

So here we have a brief where the challenge is to influence your boss to take some action. The assessors will want to see whether you can be appropriately assertive and use good arguments to win your boss over. Once again the role player will respond based on how you manage the conversation.

A good sequence to consider in conducting the meeting is as follows:

- Explain your reason for wanting the meeting.
- Ask about background to understand the relationship with VFC.
- Take Chris's perspective, say things like 'it sounds as if it was a tough negotiation'.
- Make clear the risk of doing nothing.
- Make clear the risk of delaying action: it will make the final negotiation even more difficult if the customer's expectations have not been managed.
- Provide some good arguments for Chris to use: three years of good service, new contract will still be extremely competitive.
- Get Chris to set up the meeting – say you are happy to sit in if it would help.

Dos and don'ts

Do

- Take the exercise seriously. Set yourself the objective of getting Chris to arrange the meeting this week.

- Put yourself in the shoes of the person you are meeting – not the actor… the person! How would you feel in Chris's situation? How can you make the urgency clear without sounding threatening?
- Assess reactions as the meeting progresses, ie what kinds of arguments are working or not working, and tailor your approach accordingly.
- Ask Chris how you can help.

Don't

- Keep repeating the same logical argument; if Chris is resisting, ask yourself why?
- Give up! Chris will see the light if you find the right argument.
- Leave the room until you are confident that Chris is going to take action.

Relationship to competencies

Once again, here are some typical competencies, together with the behavioural indicators, that assessors would be likely to be looking for in this exercise.

Competency	Indicators for this exercise
Achievement orientated	• Takes responsibility for winning Chris over, doesn't settle for any delay • Suggests clear actions to solve the problem • Summarises and agrees clear next steps at the end of the meeting • Gets Chris to agree to act
Influencing and persuading	• Presents the problem clearly and honestly • Explains risks and benefits honestly • Shows empathy for Chris's position • Explains why Chris is the best person to hold the meeting • Explains the risk of delay
Judgement and decision making	• Monitors Chris's reactions and responds accordingly • Seeks information about the background to better understand the issue • Provides their own opinions about why action is needed, not just presenting Alex's views • Provides sound business arguments to back their case

These three examples are quite typical of the role plays you will encounter in assessment centres. Just to remind you, here is a summary of the key things to remember in order to perform at your best in this kind of exercise:

■ Treat the exercise as 'real'. In most role plays, the first requirement is to have a good conversation that is as natural as possible: to do this you need to talk to the actor as if they were the person they are portraying.

■ Don't confuse yourself by worrying about what the actor does or doesn't know, or what questions it is appropriate for you to ask. Assume that the actor is well briefed and will be able to handle anything you throw at them.

■ Set yourself some objectives for the meeting but be willing to be flexible based on how the person you are talking to responds. Deal with the real human being in front of you rather than trying to bludgeon through a prepared agenda.

■ Based on the brief you have been given, put yourself in the shoes of the person you are meeting. Role play exercises are often trying to get at your ability to empathise.

■ Don't worry about all the information you don't have! Assessors are usually very unsympathetic to comments that start 'but in the real world I would have known all the details'. Having used the exercise many times they will know that it is perfectly possible to have the conversation based on the information provided (it is the same for all candidates) so use your experience and common sense. Role plays are very rarely about your knowledge, they are about your interpersonal behaviour.

IN A NUTSHELL

■ Role plays are one of the most commonly used assessment centre exercises because they give the assessors the chance to see how you handle tricky interpersonal situations.

■ Make sure you read the brief carefully. Be sure you understand what a good outcome to the meeting looks like.

■ Always treat the situation as 'real'. Don't think of it as a role play, be yourself and let the actor do the acting.

■ Treat the person you are talking to as you would want to be treated, look for clues to how they are feeling, what they are worrying about, just as you would in a real life conversation.

■ Take responsibility and make your personal commitment to a good outcome clear.

6 PRACTICE EXERCISES – GROUP EXERCISES

This chapter will take you through the important dos and don'ts of different kinds of group exercise. Most assessment centres contain a group exercise of some kind so it is important to understand how they work and how to do your best. You will learn about:

■ different kinds of group exercise

■ your impact and performance during the exercise

■ examples of group exercises and how to handle them.

How to approach the group exercises

Meetings are a common aspect of business life and so group exercises, usually simulating a meeting of some kind, are a very common feature of assessment centres. They also give the assessors a good sample of your interpersonal behaviour. To recap, typical formats for group exercises include the following:

- **Open-ended group exercises.** All members of the group will be given the same short brief or topic to discuss.
- **Assigned role group exercises.** As above except that one group member in turn will be asked to lead or 'chair' the discussion.
- **Information-sharing group discussion.** All group members have the same basic brief, but each person has additional or slightly varying information to bring to the table as part of the discussion.
- **Conflicting information or agenda group discussion.** Each member of the group is asked to debate or argue from a slightly different viewpoint. For example, it may be a discussion about who to appoint to a particular job and each of you may have been asked to argue the case for a particular candidate based on background information you have been given.
- **Task-based exercises.** Here you are asked to collaborate with others to perform a physical task of some kind, for example building something.

Group discussion exercises are always about more than simply who does the most talking or who leads the discussion. Assessors will be looking for evidence in relation to a number of different competencies (driven as ever by the assessment matrix) so as before it makes sense for you to think holistically about the requirements of these exercises.

This said, and more so than in other exercises, your personal levels of social confidence and your verbal fluency are likely to have a big impact on your 'natural' behaviour in this kind of exercise. If you are talkative, socially poised and the kind of person who is happy to just throw your opinions on to the table, then you are likely to be giving the assessors a lot of material to work with when it comes to assessing your contribution – good or bad! If on the other hand you are less confident, preferring to speak only when you have something specific to contribute and are generally more comfortable taking a back seat during open forum discussion, then you will be making it harder for the assessors to take a view.

While our general advice throughout an assessment centre is to be yourself as much as possible, there is no doubt that your contribution rate (quite simply the proportion of the available air time that you get) does make a difference to how you are likely to be evaluated during a group discussion exercise. Regardless of specific competencies and behavioural indicators, assessors will be noticing the following:

- how much you speak
- the quality of what you are saying
- body language
- how consistent your contribution is across the whole discussion
- how you are treating other group members
- your contribution to managing the group, e.g. time keeping and keeping the group on track.

Thinking about your personal style, and how talkative or verbally fluent you are, you should look at this list and identify where you see any personal assets or risks in terms of your behaviour. For example, consider the following:

- **How much do you speak?** Is the risk that you will talk too much or too little? In general this risk manifests itself in two ways: people being over-polite and not wanting to appear too pushy with the result that you get a lacklustre discussion; or people fighting for air time and appearing competitive rather than collaborating. Regardless of your 'natural' style you need to be monitoring the discussion and assessing whether you are saying a lot more or a lot less than the other group members.
- **The quality of what you are saying.** This said, don't speak just for the sake of it! The brief will have been carefully designed to be fair to everyone so chances are that your knowledge/opinions/ideas are just as valid as everyone else's around the table. Try to keep on topic (unless you strongly believe that the discussion is heading in the wrong direction) rather than throwing in random ideas or opinions. Try and build on what other people are saying, and use questions as a way of getting yourself heard. If you don't have a particularly strong view on the issue being discussed you can still signal that you are engaged and interested by asking questions like:
  - Are there any other factors we should be considering?
  - Does anyone else have a strong view on this?
  - I'm wondering if there is any other angle we should be thinking about.

- **Body language.** The assessors will be watching carefully to see what your body language is 'saying' about you, most particularly in terms of how engaged you are with the discussion and with the other group members. Your posture (leaning forwards or leaning backwards, your eye contact), are you attending to whoever is speaking (rather than staring at the table) and your other signals such as head nodding, all have the potential to tell assessors that you are playing a full part in the discussion even when you are not speaking.
- **Consistency of contribution.** Ideally you should aim to be making regular contributions throughout the discussion rather than dipping in and out sporadically or speaking for a long time and then being silent for long periods. Assessors are trained to watch out for and to time periods of non-contribution so it is much better to keep your contribution 'ticking over' rather than with big peaks and troughs.
- **How you treat other group members.** You will obviously avoid being rude or abrupt with other group members (this does not mean that you can't be assertive) but assessors will also be looking for other examples of your interpersonal behaviour. For example,
  - Do you bring others into the discussion, deliberately seeking the opinion of anyone who is quieter?
  - Do you provide positive 'strokes' to other team members, congratulating them for good ideas?
  - Do you challenge 'bad' behaviour from other group members, for example 'hang on Jenny, Peter was trying to finish the point he was making'?
  - How do you react when you are challenged? Do you sound defensive or can you take the challenge in the spirit in which it was intended?
- **Your contribution to group process.** In group discussions where you have not been assigned any specific role (in other words where no one has been told that it is their job to chair or lead the meeting) the assessor will be looking for the amount of time and effort you put into managing or steering the group to achieve a good result. You can contribute very effectively to the group process simply by operating as a member of the team. However, we are a democratic nation and the early stages of a group discussion often consist of the group members deciding who will do what! The two roles that are most often discussed in this situation are 'who will take notes?' (the scribe role – either on paper or possibly standing at a flip chart or white board); the second is the role of timekeeper, reminding the group how

much progress they are making in relation to the time available. Both of these roles have the potential to help you shine but they also hold risks so think carefully before you accept either job. If you decide to be the timekeeper then don't let this role sideline you: make sure you are still an active contributor, and still do a good job as timekeeper! After all you took the job on so the assessors will not be impressed if you do it badly. If you take on the job of scribe, you have the opportunity to play a very active role by shaping the discussion, summarising and checking that the group is delivering what is required. The risk comes if you limit yourself to just writing down what you are told; you might feel you are being busy but you will be limiting the amount of evidence you are giving the assessors.

DISCRETIONARY BEHAVIOUR!

In group exercises one of the things that will colour the assessor's opinion of your performance is your discretionary behaviour – in other words what you chose to do or chose not to do. Do you step up to take responsibility even though no one is telling you to do it? Do you settle for a discussion that is meandering aimlessly or do you do something about it? How proactive are you in setting a direction for the group? How energetically are you working to deliver whatever the task is? You have a choice about all of these things and the assessors will be interested in how you exercise that choice.

Example group exercise 1 – open-ended/no assigned role

Brief

You will shortly be joining with three of your colleagues to discuss the topic described below. You will have 40 minutes for your discussion.

You and your colleagues are the grant-awarding committee of Valebridge Chamber of Commerce. The Chamber of Commerce represents local business throughout the Valebridge area and you have some 220 members ranging from large insurance companies to small local traders.

Each year the Chamber of Commerce donates a sum of money to charity and the job of your committee is to decide how this money is to be spent. By the end of your meeting you should have firm decisions about how much money is to be allocated to the eligible charities you have chosen. How the money is to be allocated is entirely up to you: you can spread the money across several organisations if you wish or, if you prefer, can give the money to only one charity. Each charity has made a request for a particular sum but you are not obliged to give them this amount. The amount of money available for you to allocate is £63,000.

The executive committee of the Chamber of Commerce has asked you to bear in mind the following guidelines.

■ There should be a strong emphasis on arts funding this year given that they have received very little support in the previous two years.
■ Charities with strong local connections and strong local visibility within Valebridge should receive preference.
■ Charities where the Chamber of Commerce is providing all the funding should be preferred because of the greater publicity exposure.

The charities that have made requests for funding are as follows, in each case any relevant notes from the Chamber of Commerce charities office are attached.

Valebridge Youth Theatre
Request for £30,000 to support refurbishment of the Market Theatre.

Notes: this is a well-thought-of local amateur theatre group which does good work with young people across the locality. Refurbishment is urgently needed and they are seeking funding from a large number of organisations – they need something like £100,000 in all. We gave them £10,000 last year to replace the lighting system.

St Margaret's Hospice
Request for £25,000 to support installation of new televisions in each guest room.

Notes: while the hospice is slightly outside the Valebridge area they are nationally known for the excellence of care they provide. The sum requested will cover the total cost of installation and we will get full credit as a 'Friend' of the Hospice.

Art in Action

Request for £60,000 to support the commissioning of two public sculptures in Valebridge Town Centre.

Notes: Art in Action are a national artistic foundation but this year they have gained agreement from the renowned sculptor Miles Griffiths, who lives locally, to deliver two sculptures reflecting local life. The town is currently very short of any public art of this kind.

Vale Drug Awareness

Request for £45,000 to support the continuation of their schools visit programme.

Notes: We gave them part funding last year (£15,000) and now they are asking if we can provide full funding; their other sponsors have pulled out and unless the money is forthcoming they will not be able to continue their good work.

Valebridge Museum

Request for £28,000 to re-open the fine art gallery.

Notes: this gallery has been closed for the last eight months because of the condition of the ceiling: it needs substantial repair. The gallery houses the Sloan Collection of Pre-Raphaelite paintings, which is recognised to be the best collection outside London. They are willing to re-name the gallery to reflect whoever provides the funds.

Homeless

Request for £10,000 to support their continuing work with homeless people, specifically provision of hostel accommodation.

Notes: while Homeless is a national charity, there is a hostel in Valebridge though they are unwilling to guarantee that the funds would be spent on this particular hostel.

Able Art

Request for £30,000 to hire two new art teachers for the home visit programme.

Notes: this regional charity specialises in providing art training and materials for people with disabilities, especially those with mobility problems who find it difficult to access other forms of adult education. This charity is a particular favourite of the MD of Axon Insurance – the largest member of the Chamber of Commerce.

Valebridge School PTA

Request for £17,000 to refurbish the science and design block at the sixth form college.

Notes: The Parent Teacher Association collects a lot of money through its own efforts but needs sponsorship from other organisations to raise the £47,000 they need to refurbish the science block. Clearly a lot of our members have children at the school and this would help them to see a direct return for their Chamber of Commerce membership.

You have 40 minutes to decide how you wish to allocate the £63,000. You should also prepare a short statement explaining how you have come to your decisions.

This brief is quite typical of the open-ended discussion type. There is clearly no right or wrong answer to the challenge, just lots of different ways of carving up the available resource. So, it is a problem-solving exercise with a tight time deadline. You have some guidelines to follow but the key to success is going to be how well, and how quickly, the group gets to grips with the task.

You will typically be given at least a few minutes to prepare for this kind of exercise so how should you use the time?

Clearly you will want to read through the brief and consider the various options you have (perhaps doing a rough estimate of how many of the projects you can support given the available funds) but you should be devoting a good chunk of your preparation time to thinking about **how** the group can best approach the problem. In a decision-making task like this one groups often go wrong by not giving enough time (or indeed any time) to agreeing a strong process for getting to the result. Failure to do this means that the group can spend a lot of time in silence as they desperately wade through the information, and this does not impress the assessors.

Key process points to consider during your prep time are as follows:

- Get the group to agree clear criteria up front. You have been given guidelines but you will need additional clarification of how you will decide if a project is worthy of support. Fail to do this and the discussion will go round and round in circles.
- Someone needs to keep an eye on the arithmetic to make sure that you are not overspending.
- How are you going to manage the time? There are eight projects to consider, you only have 40 minutes, and if you start going through them one by one you need very tight time control – max three minutes each. What typically happens is that you spend 15 minutes discussing the first two projects, realise that this approach won't work, and then waste time coming up with a different approach. You have to manage time right from the start.
- You need to be able to justify your decisions, ideally showing that you have applied consistent criteria/rules. This task would be very easy if you just chose projects at random. The assessors will want to see the group being consistent, objective and fair, so you need to build in time to provide your explanation of how you reached your decisions.

If you have thought about these in advance you will be able to start the meeting off with a flourish. Clearly the detail of the task will be different for any given group exercise. The key message to remember here is **give time to thinking about the process and don't settle for the first idea that someone puts on the table**, for example 'I think we should just go through them one by one'. Challenge yourself and the group to come up with at least a couple of ideas for how to approach the task before you just leap in.

Dos and don'ts

Do
- Use your prep time well to think about the process of the discussion as well as the subject matter.
- Try to contribute consistently throughout the discussion but avoid side tracking the group with random ideas or opinions.

■ Make sure that there is a clear rationale for the group's decisions.
■ Think about how you are treating other group members. Take opportunities to ask questions and bring quieter people into the discussion.

Don't
■ Be competitive with other group members. You are all in this together to solve the problem, cooperative behaviour is likely to go down much better than fighting for space!
■ Be defensive or sulk if someone disagrees with you or if your ideas are not immediately adopted: stay with the discussion.
■ Take on any specific role, for example scribe, unless you are happy that you can acquit this role well and still maintain your contribution to the discussion.

Relationship to competencies

Here are some typical competencies, together with the behavioural indicators, that assessors would likely be looking for in this kind of group discussion exercise.

Competency	Indicators for this exercise
Energy and drive	• Takes responsibility for getting a result throughout the meeting • Suggests alternatives if the group is getting stuck • Seeks to motivate the group, encourages them • Is an active contributor throughout the meeting
Analytical thinking	• Assimilates the information quickly and accurately • Identifies, or helps the group to identify, clear decision criteria • Weighs up all the different viewpoints influencing the decision
Influencing and persuading	• Presents ideas and opinions politely and clearly • Asks questions to understand other people's point of view • Promotes ideas consistently but in line with the discussion • Uses rational persuasion, builds a logical argument
Team leadership	• Provides ideas for team process, suggests methods for delivering the task • Provides direction and steers the discussion throughout the exercise not just at the start • Helps the group to make decisions, brings things to a conclusion • Directs and manages the discussion without domineering

Example group exercise 2 – shared information

A common variation on the discussion theme is to provide participants with slightly different information or additional information as part of their brief. In other words, only one candidate around the table has this unique information. The main reasons for doing this are to make sure that each participant has something specific to bring to the discussion and to build some potential competitiveness into the task. It also raises the complexity of the task because only by sharing information well can the task be accomplished.

The following section gives you additional information that should be considered alongside the information you already have in Example 1.
In other words, each candidate has **one** of the following pieces of information that they will bring to the table when the discussion starts.

Candidate A

In addition to the general information in this brief, you have been provided with the following comment from the Chair of the Chamber of Commerce.

I know the charity committee is meeting today and I thought I ought to let you know that I bumped into the head of the PTA today. She made it clear that a number of parents who are also Chamber of Commerce members have said that they are confident that the PTA will get the funding. I don't know where they have got this idea from – has someone been raising false expectations? We could have some annoyed members on our hands if we don't give them the funding.

Candidate B

In addition to the general information in this brief, you have been provided with the following comment from the Treasurer of the Chamber of Commerce.

As part of your discussion about the allocation of charitable funds I think you might also need to consider the following. I know that you have already had the guideline that we would prefer projects where we are providing all the funding – not part funding. I have recently spoken to our accountants and it seems that where we provide all the funding there are significant tax benefits. The effect of this is that where we provide all the funding, we can effectively

offer 10% more money because of the tax we will be able to claim back. You
might need to consider this as part of your discussion.

Candidate C

In addition to the general information in this brief, you have been provided with
the following comment from Lady Jane Stuart, Chair of Art in Action.

I know that you are meeting today to consider fund allocation and I thought
you might like to know the following. I was recently speaking to the Chair of
the Rural Art Commission (who also happens to be a personal friend of Miles
Griffiths) who suggested that the presence of two of his sculptures could have
a major impact on whether the RAC would release some of its funds for the
Valebridge area. This could be worth anything up to £250,000 so I thought you
might like to consider this as a relevant factor.

Candidate D

In addition to the general information in this brief, you have been provided
with the following comment from Dr Salem Neshman, Head of Vale Drug
Awareness.

I know that you are making your funding decisions today and I just wanted
to make you aware of how desperate the situation is with regard to this kind
of education within Valebridge. We have clear evidence from independent
research that our initiatives have driven down drug abuse by over 10% over
the last ten years (the direct opposite of the national trend) and we feel it would
be a tragedy for this good work to be undone by a lack of funds. We know that
times are hard but I would make a special plea for our project. You really are
our last option to keep this initiative going.

You can see how this additional information has the potential to make your task
much more complicated. How much weight should you give to this additional
information? How quickly and efficiently does the group share the information?
These questions will have a major impact on how the discussion goes.

The basic principles for helping the group to establish a good process for decision making (as described above) still apply. However, there are some additional points worth bearing in mind to help with this scenario:

- It is a good idea to check at the start of the meeting if everyone has the same information or if anyone has additional information.
- Don't feel that you have to act on the specific information you have, in other words defending a particular position, simply factor the additional data into the discussion in the same way you would all the other information and don't get competitive about it.
- Keep track of the extra information, because only one of you will have this information written down it is really important that you find a way of sharing it amongst the group, otherwise you will find yourself having to constantly refer back to the individual brief. Think about summarising it on a flip chart so that it is visible to all.

Dos and don'ts

Do

- Use your prep time to consider your piece of additional information along with the rest of the brief.
- Think about whether the additional information has an impact on the criteria you will apply in order to reach a decision.
- Consider ways in which all the information can be pulled together. If you have additional information you can bet that the other candidates do as well.

Don't

- Be cagey or secretive about the additional information.
- Become defensive about the position implied by the additional information, factor it in with all the available data.
- Be fooled into thinking that there is a right or wrong answer to the challenge. The key thing the assessors are looking for is your contribution to the process.

Relationship to competencies

In addition to the competencies you have already seen for the previous example, here are some additional competencies and behavioural indicators that this kind of exercise might attract.

Competency	Indicators for this exercise
Energy and drive	• Takes responsibility for getting the information shared quickly • Persists in trying to find a way through the complexity of the exercise
Analytical thinking	• Assimilates the information quickly and accurately • Thinks about the data as a whole, is not unduly swayed by any one piece of information • Helps the group to identify an analytical process for the exercise, for example considering the guidelines first and only then factoring in additional information

Example group exercise 3 – assigned role

There are two main types of assigned role exercise. One is where you are all given the same brief (as in the above examples) but where you are specifically told to lead the meeting or to act as the chair of the meeting. If you are given this role, the meeting will usually be shorter. (Think about the timetable, all participants will have to have a go at the leadership role). All the rules I have discussed so far still apply if you are given the job of leading the meeting but there are some additional steps you can take to deliver the role well.

■ Take responsibility by maintaining control of the process. This doesn't mean that you have to come up with all the ideas, indeed it's important that you get contributions from the group, but do stay in charge of the timing and move the discussion on if time is being wasted.
■ Allocate tasks to other group members, for example timekeeper or scribe, don't try and do everything yourself.
■ Keep an overview of progress, don't get sucked into the detail to the point that you lose sight of the overall objective.
■ Manage the group, make sure that everyone is contributing, seek the opinion of any quieter group members.
■ Consider the task, thought, people model. If you have been put in a leadership role, chances are that the assessors will be evaluating your performance across all of these areas.

Assessors don't like wasting data: if you are in an assigned role group discussion but are not the leader, the assessors will still be evaluating your performance – this is not the time to sit back and take a rest! Be guided by all the hints and advice I have provided so far about behaviour in group exercises.

The second (and probably more common) form of assigned role exercise is where you alone are given all or most of the information and have to share this with the group before leading the discussion to resolve the issue. These are sometimes called briefing exercises. Here is an example of this kind of exercise.

Brief

You will shortly be taking part in a group discussion exercise where you will need to present information to the group and then seek their support in coming to a decision. The other group members do not have any information about this topic so you will need to introduce the information to them clearly.

You now have 15 minutes to prepare for the exercise. The discussion itself will last for a maximum of 20 minutes and you should plan your use of time accordingly. You should aim to come to a decision by the end of this time.

Cowbridge General Hospital Buildings Committee

You are about to lead a short meeting of the buildings committee to discuss the following challenge.

The head of site services at the hospital (responsible for all the hospital's buildings, services and grounds) has recently completed a structural survey of the hospital and has found the following problems.

The hospital's east wing, which houses three medical wards on three stories, was built only two years ago but is showing signs of structural problems. There are rumours, nothing more at this stage, that the builder responsible is about to be taken to court by Valebridge Council because of another building (the local library) which is also experiencing structural problems. The library has had to be closed on safety grounds because it is suspected that substandard materials were used in its construction. The result is that wall panels are loose and in danger of falling off, cracks have appeared in the stairwells and there is evidence of the foundations subsiding because the pillars used to support the structure were not properly drilled.

The head of site services now says that evidence of similar problems has arisen at the hospital. Specifically, some of the external cladding panels are loose and in danger of falling off, an area outside of the hospital has had to be cordoned off for the safety of the public. At the same time there is evidence that some of the concrete and steel pillars that support the lift shaft in the east wing are starting to lean. They are currently still within the building regulation tolerances and while sensors say that the movement has slowed over the last six months, they are still moving.

The head of site services is asking that you consider a gradual closing of the east wing in order that a full investigation can take place. He points out that a partial investigation could be conducted with the building still being occupied but that even this would be very disruptive to patients and staff, as it would involve significant excavation and drilling which would be noisy and create a lot of dust. There is a risk that the partial investigation would still not provide a conclusive answer as to the safety of the building. This is why he would prefer to close the building and investigate properly – it would be faster and would enable any remedial work that was needed to be done without any further disruption. He estimates that the building would need to be closed for three months, longer if significant remedial building work was needed. The partial investigation option would take longer than this because of the need to work around patients and staff though it is hard to estimate how much longer until the medical teams have been consulted to explore how much disruption is acceptable.

The head of site services has not yet escalated the problem to the hospital administration as a whole because he wants the view of your committee before setting in motion a train of events that would have a significant impact on the hospital's ability to deliver its services. He points out that once the medical teams hear that there are rumours of possible safety issues, there could be pressure to close the east wing immediately.

It is February and the hospital's busiest time. The beds in the east wing are currently 95% occupied and closing the wing quickly would cause severe disruption. Patients would need to be relocated to other hospitals in the region and this in itself could have a detrimental effect on their health outcomes. It would also be likely to create very unwelcome negative publicity. The head of site services is asking that you consider a phased closure of the wing, one ward at a time in order to minimise the impact on patients and staff. On this *basis it would take about three months to empty the building completely; this would help the site investigation team because it would enable them to start their work when the weather was better, this in turn enabling them to complete the work more quickly.*

As the hospital's buildings committee it is your responsibility to make firm recommendations to the hospital administration as to the best way forward. You have twenty minutes to reach your decision.

A knotty problem then, how should you go about resolving it?

As well as your behaviour in the meeting, one key to shining in this kind of exercise is using your preparation time well. As well as familiarising yourself with the subject matter of the exercise you should also be thinking about two other things:

■ How to inform the group about the issues clearly and succinctly.
■ How you are going to lead the group to help you with the problem.

There is a temptation to focus on the information you have and to use all the preparation time to make up your own mind about what the best option is. However, bear in mind what the assessors are looking for. If all they were interested in was your judgement about the best way forward, then they would have asked you to make a written recommendation but this is a group discussion exercise. By definition then, the assessors are going to be interested in how you share the information and how you run the discussion. Typically

---

DECIDE TO DECIDE

When the exercise brief asks you to make a decision – make a decision! You will seldom have all the information you would like and there is always a temptation to avoid coming to a conclusion by asking for more data or by saying that you will meet again at some point in the future when more information is available. The risk is that this will give the assessors clear negative evidence about you in relation to competencies such as 'energy and drive' and 'judgement and decision making'.

---

there is no right or wrong answer to this kind of challenge so don't tie yourself in knots trying to find the perfect solution – chances are there isn't one. Get the group to help you find a rational answer based on the limited available information.

How to inform the group

Clearly the details of how you go about this will depend on the complexity of the information you have been given but there are some general principles that will serve you well in this kind of exercise:

- As you prepare, note down the key points of information you have and make sure you distinguish between hard facts and supposition. In relation to the example exercise your notes might include the following:
  - Facts: external wall panels are loose; this is unsafe for members of the public; pillars in the lift shaft are moving but are not currently unsafe; two kinds of investigation are possible; the wards in the east wing are nearly full; closing them will cause disruption; administration and medical teams do not currently know the scale of the problem
  - Supposition: substandard materials might have been used in construction; the medical teams would respond badly and overreact; patients might suffer if they had to be moved.
- Consider how to get the key points across quickly, and plan how you are going to pass on the information. **Don't just read them the brief: it will take too long!** You need to find a way of summarising, by highlighting what you see as the most important issues, but making sure you give them the full picture. Remember to make sure you explain to the group what the task is, namely that you have to come up with recommendations. You should aim to use no more than 20% of your available time to present the information, so in this scenario you have to get the key information across in less than five minutes! There will be inevitable clarifying questions from the group so consider how much time you will allow for this; it is surprisingly easy to use up too much of the meeting in just getting the facts straight leaving you little time to discuss the options. Your brief to the group might start something like this:

  "OK everyone, this is the situation: we are the building committee of Cowbridge General Hospital and we have to make an urgent decision about how to handle a construction safety problem. We have to come up with clear recommendations by the end of our meeting. I'm going to lay out the

facts and it might be an idea if you make some notes so that I don't have to go over the information."

■ As part of your preparation plan how to lay out the main dilemmas the group has to consider; use these as a way of summarising at the end of your briefing time, for example:

"OK then, the main issues as I see them are as follows: do we see a safety issue that would cause us to close the whole of the east wing immediately or do we follow the suggestion of a phased closure? Do we close the east wing at all or do we go for the option of a partial investigation? How and when do we get the administration and medical teams involved in the issue?"

How are you going to lead the group?

At the start of this example I reminded you about the importance of managing the **process** of the group discussion. The assessors will be watching you to see that you are taking responsibility for this element of the task as well as for the contribution you personally make to reaching a decision. In this exercise, the ultimate decision will be yours. By all means check for the consensus of the group but make sure that you are happy that the final decision is rational and defensible in terms of the facts and the discussion you have had.

Clearly, once you have briefed them, you will be asking the group for their views, ideas and suggestions. It is also a good idea to ask someone to keep track of the time so that you can focus on steering the discussion.

Remember, good behaviours to show are:

■ seeking views
■ making sure everyone contributes
■ referring to people by name
■ keeping the discussion on the main issues
■ politely managing people who are going off track/talking too much
■ making sure that the task is achieved – namely that you reach a clear decision.

Bad behaviours to be avoided are:

■ dismissing other people's views out of hand
■ getting into a debate with one other individual at the expense of the group as a whole

- being rude or too abrupt
- spending too much time defending your view at the expense of hearing others
- not being actively involved at all times.

As I mentioned earlier, the task, thought, people model is a good guide as you manage the discussion:

- **Task:** is the group on track, is the task clear, is time being well used, are you going to deliver the objective?
- **Thought:** are you encouraging creativity, are judgements well founded, are decisions sensible given the facts?
- **People:** is everyone engaged, are you maximising their contributions, and are you encouraging and motivating people?

Dos and don'ts

Do
- Use your prep time well to think about the content and the process.
- Adhere to the instructions, so if you are asked for a decision, make sure you give them one.
- Stay actively involved, not domineering, but making sure that your leadership of the group is visible to the assessors.

Don't
- Use all your prep time trying to solve the problem yourself without considering the group.
- Try to bulldoze your own views through without encouraging contributions from the group.
- Simply dump the problem on the group and then take a back seat – your task isn't finished until you have steered the group to a good decision!

Relationship to competencies

Here are some typical competencies, together with the behavioural indicators, that assessors would be likely to be looking for in an assigned role group discussion exercise.

Competency	Indicators for this exercise
Energy and drive	• Takes responsibility for getting a result throughout the meeting • Moves the group on if they are getting stuck • Seeks to motivate the group, encourages them • Steers the group to a clear decision or recommendations, does not put off the decision
Analytical thinking	• Briefs the group accurately, does not miss out important information • Identifies, or helps the group to identify, the main factors that have to be considered • Weighs up all the different factors and viewpoints influencing the decision
Team leadership	• Provides ideas for team process, suggests methods for delivering the task • Provides direction and steers the discussion throughout the exercise not just at the start • Helps the group to make decisions, brings things to a conclusion • Directs and manages the discussion without domineering

IN A NUTSHELL

■ Group exercises are a very common element of assessment centres and one where your own personality and interpersonal 'style' is an important factor that needs to be managed if you are to perform well.

■ Take responsibility. Whether you have been given the job of leading the group or not, make sure that you are working to deliver the group's objective. Don't be tempted to take a back seat.

■ Think about process as well as content. The assessors will be at least as interested in *how* the group is discussing as they are in *what* the group is discussing.

■ Contribute consistently throughout the discussion and avoid long silences. Use questions as a way of staying in the discussion if you don't have a specific point you want to make at that moment in time.

■ Use your preparation time well to think holistically about the exercise. Remember task, thought, people because the assessors will probably be looking at your contribution in terms of all three!

7 PRACTICE EXERCISES – PRESENTATIONS

This chapter will help you to think through the basics of presenting well as part of an assessment centre. While not aiming to cover every aspect of presentation skills, this chapter will:

- explain the main kinds of presentation you are likely to encounter in an assessment centre

- explore the best ways of structuring your presentation

- help you to get the content right

- explore key aspects of your delivery style as a presenter.

Presentation skills – the basics

A lot of organisations put a high value on presentation skills and as a result, presentation exercises often get built into assessment centres. From a purist point of view presentation exercises are often not the best way to get at competencies (except for social confidence and verbal fluency) because it is difficult for assessors to evaluate content without being influenced by the manner of the delivery. An assessment centre is probably not the best time to point this out to assessors, however, so in this section I will try and help you to do a good job in terms of both content and delivery! The good news is that presentation skills are very trainable, meaning that anyone can get a lot better at them with guidance and practice.

This section cannot duplicate all the advice that you would find in a dedicated book on presentation skills but it can ensure that you have the basic structures and principles that will help you to do well in this kind of exercise.

There are a variety of ways in which a presentation exercise can crop up in an assessment centre. Some of the most common ones are:

- presenting on a topic that you have been asked to prepare in advance of the assessment centre
- presenting back the conclusions of a case study exercise that you have completed previously as part of the assessment centre
- presenting back as part of a group.

Because of the constraints of an assessment centre timetable, any presentation you are asked to make will usually be short, probably no longer than 15 minutes and often shorter, so it is important to consider how to get your message across in this timescale.

The principles across all these variations are the same, so the example that follows will use the format of you being asked to present back as the result of a previous exercise. In this case we will use the example of the Cowbridge General Hospital assigned role group discussion from the previous chapter.

First, however, I will cover some general advice about presentations under the headings of structure, content and style.

Structure

The structure of your presentation needs to support the overall purpose you have in making the presentation. Think about **why** you are being asked to present this information out loud rather than simply giving the assessors some written output to consider?

In an ideal world, a presentation needs to add some value that the assessors would not get from just reading your ideas, so the structure you put on your presentation needs to give you the chance to add this value. At the risk of giving you a sweeping generalisation, the most common set of attributes that assessors will be looking for are around whether you can be **logically persuasive**. So your structure should serve this end.

At the same time you should be aiming to make your presentation build into an interesting story (as well as being logically persuasive). Bear in mind that the poor overworked assessors will be watching a number of presentations on the same topic so it is worth thinking about how to make yours stand out. So, structurally, what helps?

Broad structure

'Tell them what you are going to tell them, then tell them, then tell them what you have told them' is old but good advice when it comes to structuring a presentation, even a short one! In other words do the following:

- First: set out the presentation explaining what you are going to cover and the structure you are going to follow. Be clear about what you are or are not going to include and your rationale for doing so.
- Second: present your conclusions/ideas/recommendations following the structure you have described above.
- Third: summarise your presentation giving the assessors a clear reminder of your main points and the conclusions you have come to.

Given this overall advice you will often be offered some additional guidance about what the assessors are expecting to see in the presentation, and sometimes this guidance can be quite specific in order to allow the assessors to make their evaluations more easily. The key message here is to follow the instructions. If you have been asked to present based on specific headings or using a specific structure then stick to it – if you start playing fast and loose with their structure you will just make it harder for them to do their job.

Some examples of the kind of instruction you might be given are provided below. They all vary in terms of how much scope they give you to develop your own structure as opposed to following theirs.

Example presentation instructions

A. *You will have ten minutes to present the results of your discussion to the assessors: please make sure that you cover both the process you went through and your overall recommendations. The assessors will ask any follow-up questions at the end of your presentation.*

B. *Later today you will have the chance to present your ideas to the assessors; please use the following structure for your presentation:*
   - *The criteria you used to make your decision*
   - *The options you considered*
   - *Your final recommendation*

C. *Please present back to the assessors highlighting what you believe to be the most important elements of the decision you made.*

You can see the range of options here, some instructions constrain you a lot, others give you a lot of rope! If you are given the kind of wide open brief as described in example C, then it is all the more important that you use the following format for structuring the presentation:

- tell them what you are going to tell them
- tell them
- tell them what you have told them.

The instructions they give you also provide some clues about what the assessors are looking for. As a general rule of thumb, the more specific the instructions are, the more likely it is that the assessors are trying to get at specific competencies such as decision making or how you analyse. (In example B above it is clear that they want you to structure your presentation in a way that reveals the thought process you went through.) The more general the instructions are, the more likely it is that the assessors are interested in your influencing style, how well you can construct an argument and how confidently you make your case. (It clearly makes sense that if they want to get an assessment of how well you can construct an argument, they are not going to tell you exactly how to do it!)

Regardless of the instructions you receive, it is important to remember that the typically short timescale means that you have to keep your presentation simple. In ten minutes you should not be trying to get more than two or three points across.

GET OFF THE FENCE!

If the exercise brief asks you to make recommendations, then make recommendations! Present the pros and cons by all means but you will need to jump off the fence at some point and give the assessors your best option for a way forward. It can be tempting to be non-committal as a way of avoiding a 'wrong' answer but this is usually a mistake. Exercises of this kind seldom have a clear-cut right answer and all you will be doing is showing the assessors that you are indecisive!

Detailed structure

Clearly, the details of the topic on which you are presenting will have an impact on the structure you choose for your presentation. One tool which can help you to ensure that you have considered all aspects of the problem should already be familiar to you from Chapter 1 – the Radar model which reminds us to consider the 'people, task, thought' aspects of any problem we are considering. If we take as an example the presentation based on the Cowbridge General Hospital brief we saw in the Group exercise example 3, pages 114–116 (you might want to re-read this now to remind yourself), then you will see how this approach helps to make sure that all aspects of the problem have been considered. Look at the following as a possible structure.

Tell them what you are going to tell them

Outline the process you went through and the recommendations you arrived at including the following:

- The viewpoint of relevant stakeholders (PEOPLE)
- The facts of the problem (TASK)
- Potential ideas, solutions and recommendations (THOUGHT)

Tell them

- The opinions and views that you considered (PEOPLE)
- The issues, options, risks and outcomes involved (TASK)
- Ideas, solutions and a recommended way forward (THOUGHT)

Tell them what you have told them

Give them a short summary:

- Views (PEOPLE)
- Facts of the problem (TASK)
- Your recommendations (THOUGHT)

The point of using the task, thought, people model is that it helps you to ensure that you have not left anything out. This is important because assessors will be interested in seeing if you have considered all aspects of the problem and that you have taken an objective view. It is all too easy to select and present those aspects of the problem and those facts that support your conclusion. There is a big risk in doing this – bear in mind that the assessors know all the facts and they will judge you poorly if they think you are presenting a one-sided argument.

Content

What is everyone else going to say? If you use this as your starting question then it will prompt you to think of ways of making your presentation stand out as more interesting than the others. Clearly, as I mentioned above, you have to answer the requirements of the brief you have been given but you should still think about the presentation as an opportunity to show that you can build a persuasive argument that is well structured but that also contains the right stuff!

I mentioned at the start that you will typically have a very limited time for your presentation during an assessment centre, so in terms of content, the challenge will often be one of having to edit down the available information. 'Only put in what is essential' is good advice when designing any presentation but it is even more important given the constraints of an assessment centre.

You will have already noted the importance of presenting a balanced argument rather than being selective with the facts or massaging the information to support your particular conclusion. Assessors will spot this instantly (they know the material backwards) and will probably penalise you for it.

Media

You may also be given options about how you present information. In other words, whether presentation media such as flip charts, white boards or PowerPoint presentation software is available.

In most cases, using some form of visual medium will improve your presentation but it needs to be used well. The best use of media in this presentation context is as a way of showing highly simplified information in bullet point form or even as single words or headings – these can serve you well as a prompt so that you can refer to your notes less.

If you are used to using a tool such as PowerPoint, the temptation is to include too much information. You should never put dense text into a slide (even though a lot of people still do), rather, treat any slides you use as a form of flip chart, just capturing main headings. Whether you are using slides or a flip chart remember the following:

- keep it simple, don't worry about design or using clip art, just be sure your media are clear
- present in a logical order
- use single words or short phrases to give headlines that you can elaborate on
- write legibly!
- use as few slides or flip chart sheets as possible, an absolute maximum of four/five for a 10-minute presentation
- never include dense text.

So, bearing in mind what I have said about structure and media, how do you get the content right? We will again use the Cowbridge General Hospital brief as our example (see pages 114–116).

Let's assume that your meeting on this topic went well and that you were able to get the group to agree on clear recommendations. Let's also assume that the presentation brief you have been given is of the open-ended variety as follows:

Following on from your meeting you have been asked to present the results of your discussion to the Hospital General Committee. You will only have ten minutes for your presentation after which time the committee members may ask follow-up questions. They are keen to understand the problem and to hear your recommendations.

The final assumption we will make is that you have chosen (or been told) to use a flip chart as a visual aid during the presentation.

Bearing in mind everything you have read so far, what should be guiding your decisions about the content of this presentation?

Simplicity

Using the structure we discussed earlier, the simplest form of content will be to provide a little background, to outline the problem or problems, to present the range of options you discussed and then to present your recommendations. The flip charts you prepare might look something like this:

Background:	The Problem:
East wing structural problems	Evidence - need more!
Safety	Risk
Evidence	Need for investigation
Expert opinion	Service delivery - 95% utilised
	Disruption vs Safety

Completeness

In presenting what is covered on these flip charts you need to make sure that you are including the whole argument. So, for example, on flip chart 2 you need to make sure that you fairly represent the debate you had in balancing disruption vs safety. But, bear in mind that completeness has to be balanced with the need to keep to the point and manage time.

You have ten minutes for the presentation, and therefore no more than two and a half minutes per flip chart is available, so how should you apportion time? Remember that you are trying to be logically persuasive and to build a story.

The climax of this story is your recommendations so you must make sure that you don't end up rushing this part of the presentation. For this presentation our suggested timing would be:

Background   1 minute
The problem   2 minutes
Options   3 minutes
Recommendations   4 minutes

This suggested timing (and of course it is never possible to time these situations to the second) puts the emphasis in the places where the assessors are likely to be most interested.

You will also demonstrate completeness in your presentation if you make it clear that you have thought through the knock-on effects of your decisions and have considered contingency plans for the options you have discussed. In our example, this takes the form of showing that you have considered the safety vs disruption dilemma and that you have discussed a plan for phased ward closure if this becomes necessary.

BE LOGICAL

Remember that the assessors are going to be interested in the logic you have applied to the problem as much as in your presentation style so make it easy for them to see the quality of your thinking.

Make it interesting!

Yours might well be the third or fourth presentation that the assessors have seen on exactly the same topic, so as well as simplicity and completeness you should also be considering your content from the point of view of its interest level. Where you can, add colour or examples based on your own experience of similar decisions – in other words try to put something of yourself into the presentation but not at the expense of clarity and completeness. How to make sure that **you** come through as part of the presentation is the subject of the next section.

Delivery style

How do you come over when you are presenting? If you don't have a clear answer to this question then you need to find out. Recording yourself or presenting in front of friends are two obvious ways in which you can resolve this but it is really important that you understand your impact in this kind of situation.

Years ago, presentation skills training used to promote a fixed approach to the performance, emphasising the importance of keeping still, keeping hand movements to a minimum, using a measured tone and so on. While you don't want to be leaping about in a distracting way, the trouble with this advice is that it can stop your personality coming through.

In terms of your presentation style, here are some questions you should ask yourself in advance of any assessment centre:

■ **How confident do you sound when presenting?**

Assessment centres can tend to over-assess verbal fluency and social confidence and nowhere is this more true than in a presentation exercise. Good assessors will try to see beyond this but it would be naïve to think that a stumbling or whispered presentation will go down as well as a confidently delivered one. Practice is the key here: you need to hear yourself speaking out loud so that you get a good sense of the pace, volume and clarity of your presentation style. It is also worth bearing in mind that pressure or nervousness will usually have the effect of damping down your usual style. So, if you are softly spoken to begin with, you may need to be alert to the need to lift your voice, even if you are only presenting to a small audience. The time to find this out is in advance of the assessment centre, not while you are attending it!

■ **Are there mannerisms or verbal habits you need to be aware of?**

Nervous laughs, throat clearing, umms, words you tend to over-use, physical 'fidgets' or odd postures will all distract the assessor so they need to be managed. You can only manage them if you know they are happening so, again, practising and getting feedback is the obvious answer. There is a careful balance you need to find here, so only try to change things if you feel that they get in the way, the risk otherwise is that you will appear self-conscious and 'stiff'.

If you need to change any of these things, give yourself plenty of time to work at it and practise. People tend to make the best impact in presentations when they appear authentic and 'comfortable in their own skins', so prepare, but don't try to change anything that will get in the way of 'you' coming across as a person.

Share your thought process

A powerful way of enhancing your authenticity is to do some of your thinking 'out loud'. One of the traps we fall into when presenting is to focus on conclusions and outcomes at the expense of telling the story about how we came to those conclusions. Stylistically, sharing your thought processes is powerful because it tells the assessors the 'working out' you have done behind the scenes. (A bit like showing an examiner your 'working notes' during a maths exam.) Phrases such as the following can really help to get your message across with more weight than just a bald statement of the facts:

- "… as part of the discussion I wondered if we were over-estimating the importance of …"
- "… at this point in the discussion I began to realise that we weren't giving enough consideration to …"
- "… I quickly realised that patient disruption was the key criterion …"
- "… I'm still concerned that we don't have enough data to reach a solid decision …"

Phrases like this show that it is **you** who is talking and that you are not just reporting back as an impartial observer.

Dealing with questions

Most presentation exercises will make time at the end for the assessors to ask you a few questions and it is well worth thinking about how you will handle these. Sometimes questions will be about genuine points of clarification, asking you to explain further something that you covered in the presentation itself. Often, however, the questions will be a 'mini' assessment of their own. In other words there will be specific competencies that they are assessing based on how you respond to challenge and how well you can think on your feet.

It is also important to recognise or to clarify when you are being asked to 'stay in role' during the questioning stage or when you are being asked to step out of character to comment on the exercise itself. Assessors should make this clear to you but it is usually pretty obvious from the kind of question you are being asked. Consider the following examples.

'In role' questions (again based on the Cowbridge General Hospital scenario):

- "What objections do you anticipate you might get from the medical teams?"
- "How will you go about considering the point of view of the patient groups?"
- "How confident are you that your recommendations will be accepted by the general committee?"

'Out of role' questions:

- "Tell us about the steps you took as you prepared your presentation?"
- "In an ideal world, what other information would you have liked as part of the exercise?"
- "If you were doing the exercise again, what would you do differently?"

Deal with questions as openly and honestly as you can (the advice already given in the interview section in Chapter 4 is all relevant here). Clearly the assessors will be interested in how well you respond to challenge and how well you can think on your feet but you should also be willing to say when you simply 'don't know'.

You may occasionally be asked questions which are specifically designed to test your willingness to push back against challenge. They may look something like these:

- "Surely you don't have enough information to make a decision at this stage. Isn't 'wait and see' the best option?"
- "Safety has to be the first priority so why on earth aren't you closing the wards straight away?"
- "Aren't you overreacting, why not just do some remedial work?"

This kind of question is often set up to be slightly confrontational, so don't take it personally! The assessors will be doing the same to everyone with the aim of testing whether you can back up your arguments without becoming defensive or losing your cool.

Your best response to this kind of question (and indeed all the questions you are likely to be asked) is to calmly explain the logic behind the decision or recommendation and to do this without being long-winded or by starting to waffle. What you should definitely *not* do is to start getting confrontational with the assessors. Responses like the following will definitely not go down well because they signal that you have lost your composure.

- "…Well what would you do then?"
- "How can you possibly think that given what I have just explained?"
- "That's easy for you to say but I'm operating with limited information here."

Group presentations

All the advice given above applies equally to group presentations but with a few additional points to be aware of. If you are being asked to present back as part of a group of two, three or four then you will obviously have even less time for your part of the presentation. All the more important then that you are succinct and that you stick to time. In a group presentation assessors may also be watching for how well you cooperate and support each other as part of the exercise, so you need to give attention to the group's performance as a whole as well as to your part of it. Some specifics to consider as part of a group presentation include the following:

- You need to 'own' the group's overall conclusion, so don't be tempted to present a contrary view. The time for this is during the preparation not during the presentation itself where you will risk appearing as disruptive or as a poor team player.
- Support and help each other. If other members of the presenting team seem to be struggling, you will make a better impression if you can help them out than if you sit and watch them struggle.
- Look interested and be attentive when the other members of the team are doing their part of the presentation. Assessors will be alert to your whole performance and not just when you are presenting your bit.

Dos and don'ts

Do

- Tell them what you are going to tell them, tell them, then tell them what you have told them.
- Think about style as well as content.
- Keep it simple.
- Use any media to present headlines not detail.
- Think about timing and the structure of your message.
- Make a clear recommendation if you have been asked to do so.

Don't

■ Try to wing it rather than putting a clear structure on what you want to say.

■ Be overly argumentative or defensive under questioning.

■ Cave in. Own the decisions or recommendations you have presented.

Relationship to competencies

Here are some typical competencies, together with the behavioural indicators, that assessors would be likely to be looking for in a presentation exercise.

Competency	Indicators for this exercise
Influencing and persuading	• Presents decisions with conviction • Builds a clear argument with a supporting rationale • Shows that the viewpoint of all relevant stakeholders has been considered • Anticipates difficult influencing challenges as part of the presentation,e.g. medical teams
Analytical thinking	• Presents a clear and logical argument using all the relevant facts • Presents options and alternatives and not just one solution • Shows they have considered fall back options and has anticipated challenges
Planning and organising	• Presents using a clear structure • Manages and uses time well during the presentation • Any media used are well presented and structured • Presentation makes reference to implementation steps and stages

IN A NUTSHELL

■ Presentation exercises are a common element of assessment centres because they give assessors a relatively efficient way of judging the output of, for example, a discussion exercise as well as seeing how well you can present and defend your arguments.

■ You need to think about your 'performance' as a whole, factoring in content and style.

■ Be clear, and always adhere to the instructions. If they recommend a structure, use it; if they specify a timescale, stick to it.

■ Keep your use of media as simple as possible.

■ Tell a story that explains the thought process you went through.

■ Include all the relevant facts, and don't try to tell a one-sided story, the assessors will see through it instantly.

■ Be as natural and authentic as you can, let your personality come through.

8 PRACTICE EXERCISES – IN TRAYS, CASE STUDIES & ANALYTICAL EXERCISES

In trays, case studies and analytical exercises are a tried and trusted element of many assessment centres and they simulate the activity of sorting through a sheaf of material and deciding how to act on the information you have been given. How they are described is much less important than following some general principles in how you approach them. In this chapter I will:

■ explain the structure of this kind of exercise

■ provide guidance on how to do well

■ give you a practice exercise to work through.

What can you expect in this type of exercise?

It is arguable how many people actually have in trays on their desks these days (most of us will rely on email more than paper), but this does not stop this kind of simulation from being popular, not least because of the versatility of these tests in giving assessors information about a number of different competencies.

One of the great selling points of assessment centres as a selection process is the realism that can be generated. As a result, a lot of in-tray or case study simulations will these days be presented electronically, often through a laptop computer rather than as a simple sheaf of papers. In practice the method of presentation makes little difference to the approach you should take to doing well in this kind of exercise. At the same time, whether the exercise is called an in tray, a case study or a business analysis exercise, the approach to doing well is the same.

Exercise content

Essentially any exercise of this kind will provide you with a lot of information relating to a number of different issues. The information will usually be presented in the form of memos, letters, emails, press clippings, etc. These might relate to one issue or, more often, relate to several different issues which you have to make sense of. The information may also come from a number of different sources so one of the earliest challenges in any exercise of this kind is to 'map' the messages so that you know who has sent you what. As mentioned above, these days it is quite common for the information to be given to you through a laptop or standalone computer. The challenge here (unless you are also provided with a printer) is that you can't physically sort the information into relevant piles containing all the items that relate to a particular issue.

This mixture of content is all part of the challenge that these exercises provide and assessors will be interested in how you handle and make sense of the material as well as in how you respond to specific items or groups of items. The example given in this section mimics the typical paper-based format.

In-tray and case study exercises are also commonly set within an overarching scenario that is common to the assessment centre as a whole.

MAKE THE EXERCISE REAL

If you want to make your practice even more realistic you might want to photocopy the pages containing the exercise items so that you can shuffle and sort the papers more easily.

At this point you might want to skip ahead to page 142 to familiarise yourself with what a typical paper-based in-tray exercise looks like.

General guidance

Use the 'Radar'

Like all assessment centre exercises, an in tray or case study will be evaluated in terms of specific competencies. It is a mistake to think that assessors will only be interested in analytical type competencies in this kind of exercise (they will usually be looking more broadly than this) so it is all the more important that you apply the 'Radar' tool to make sure that you are considering and responding to all aspects of the task. If you look at the table below you will see that 'task', 'thought' and 'people' competencies will all be demanded if you are to respond well to this kind of exercise.

Type of item	What the assessors are looking for
Checking a table of figures and pointing out errors	Accuracy in checking (Task) Pointing out the consequences (Thought) The tone and sensitivity with which the errors are reported (People)
Making a decision about where to relocate an office	That a clear decision is made (Task) That all relevant factors have been considered and explained (Thought) That the impact on staff has been considered (People)
Resolving a dispute between two departments under your control	Working with the facts to understand the problem (Task) Considering long-term impact of decisions (Thought) Considering the viewpoints of all the staff involved (People)

The simple message here is to make sure that you consider each item or cluster of items 'in the round'; this gives you the best chance of covering all the relevant bases.

Follow the instructions

The instructions you get before this kind of simulation can vary widely so it is important that you pay close attention to them. Sometimes you will be asked to respond in a particular way, for example being asked to write specific letters or emails in response to items, or you may be asked to write a synopsis explaining your priorities and the decisions you have made. Often it will be a combination of these but the key thing to remember is that the assessors can only assess what you have actually put on paper. They can't see inside your head to evaluate your intentions so make sure that you respond as requested and that you make your decisions and *the thinking that led to those decisions* as clear as possible.

Look at the 'big picture' first

When faced with a sheaf of paper or with a set of emails it is very tempting to jump straight in and start responding to the individual items, but don't! Your first task should be to scan through all the items you have been given to get an overview of all the issues you are being asked to respond to. There are two main reasons for doing this: firstly, this approach lets you assess the linkages between items and it is very likely that several items might relate to the same issue; secondly this overview lets you prioritise how you are going to spend your time.

Speaking of time, how long will this kind of exercise usually last? One hour would be typical but they can range from half an hour up to two or three hours depending on their complexity and the amount of written output you are expected to produce. One other variation to watch out for is a version where you have a fixed amount of time available but it is spread out over a number of different sessions, interspersed with other assessment centre activities. Assessment centre designers like this approach because it gives them flexibility over the timetable; be assured that you will have the same time for the exercise as everyone else, though you might get your time in different slots. For example, two blocks of thirty minutes followed by a final block of one hour. Regardless of how your time is divided up, it is worth giving at least 10%–20% of your time to getting the overview of the items as a whole. So, for a two-hour in-tray exercise it would be reasonable to spend 15 to 20 minutes on assessing the big picture. Tactically, if you are faced with an exercise where your time is split, you can only do this if you have kept your eye on the total amount of time available.

Prioritise – urgent vs important

Most in trays will contain a mixture of items which are time-urgent (where you are asked for an immediate response) and items where it is less clear that there is a 'drop-dead' deadline but where the issue itself is clearly important. From your point of view it is important to distinguish between these issues so that you don't make the mistake of only responding to the urgent 'fire-fighting' issues at the expense of the more significant issues. On the other hand you don't want to get so embroiled in the meaty issues that you miss the chance for some quick wins around the shorter time-urgent items. Make sure you prioritise bearing both of these criteria in mind.

You should also be alert to 'distracter' items which are there only to add to the challenge rather than requiring a substantive response from you. (In good in trays this kind of item is becoming less common as designers realise that they are better off giving you items that need some kind of measurable, and thus assessable, response from you.)

The in-tray example given in this section is typical of what you can expect. The in trays you encounter may be longer (both in terms of number of items and in terms of the time allowed) or shorter but the principles are exactly the same. The only difference you will find in the presentation of case study or analytical exercises is that all the items relate to one issue or decision, again the principles remain the same.

Tackle the exercise exactly as you would during an assessment centre, give yourself some space somewhere quiet and see how far you get in the available time.

In-tray example

Cowbridge General Hospital

Brief

For the purposes of this exercise you are taking the role of a senior administrator who has joined Cowbridge General Hospital at short notice. You are replacing Chris Jenner who has been taken ill at very short notice and will be away from work for the foreseeable future. As such you should assume that all matters addressed for Chris Jenner are for you to deal with.

You have been asked to pick up the outstanding items and issues that Chris Jenner was dealing with and you should respond to the issues as you see fit based on your knowledge and experience. There are nine items which need your attention. You are not assumed to have any specialist knowledge relating to the exercise but you should aim to respond in writing to all the main issues as you see them.

You have 1 hour 15 minutes to respond to the items.

Today's date is 15th October 2015.

Background: the hospital is a district general hospital opened in 1975, the hospital provides modern, purpose-built accommodation for the provision of acute health services to the local population of approximately 120,000 people. The hospital provides a comprehensive range of acute surgery and medicine for patients of all ages, including inpatient, outpatient and day services. The services include:

- Accident and Emergency
- Emergency and Elective Surgery
- Emergency Medicine
- Gynaecology, Obstetrics and Neonatal Unit
- Paediatric Services
- Main Operating Theatres and Day Surgery Unit
- Coronary Care beds
- Short Stay Unit (Patient Hotel)
- Full range of diagnostic and support services.

The staff residence at the hospital has accommodation for up to 80 single occupants and 12 units for married accommodation.

Today's date is 15th October 2015.

ITEM 1

Email

From: Dr Mary Kennet: Head of Surgery

To: Chris Jenner

Date: 14/10/2015

Hi Chris

As you know Dr Okufee is joining the team as head of Cardiac Surgery on the 16th. You did say that you were going to be able to find him and his family accommodation in the staff residence for a period of three months. I have already informed him of this but I haven't had any written confirmation from you: just wanted to make sure that there were no problems. I know how much pressure there is on the accommodation but with three children he really is going to need one of the larger units.

Mary

ITEM 2

Press Cutting
Southern Press: 10/10/2015

News today from Cowbridge General Hospital that despite a campaign for free parking at the hospital, the administrators have decided to increase the parking fees by more than 20%.

Last week a spokesman for the hospital said 'we have listened carefully to the local community and we do understand their concerns, however our current cash position means that we cannot afford to subsidise parking; we know that parking is an important convenience for visitors and patients and we still believe that our charges are well within the national guidelines'.

Patient groups have been running a very active campaign over the last few weeks demanding free parking and complaining as well that customers from a nearby supermarket regularly use the hospital car park at peak times, meaning that hospital users often find it difficult to find anywhere to park at all.

On going to press yesterday, no one from Cowbridge General Hospital was available to comment. We will continue to press them for an answer.

ITEM 3

Email

From: Bill Wayne: Head of Site Services

To: Chris Jenner

Date: 14/10/2015

Chris, I sent you the figures you asked for regarding the married accommodation on the 12th but I haven't heard back from you. It really is urgent that I can get access to Units 6 and 7 to carry out decoration and maintenance. I would be really unhappy to let them out in their current condition.

I should also tell you that I think we are going to be over our maintenance budget for this year. As you can see from the numbers, the fact that we cut back last year means that we have had to do a lot of one-off repairs and this cost has mounted up. Definitely time that you let the finance committee know that this is going to have to be a priority.

Bill

ITEM 4

Letter

Miss S Hopkins OBE
The Grange
High Street
Cowbridge
10/10/2015
To whom it may concern

Dear Sir

I am writing to make a strong complaint about the treatment I have received from Ace Parking, the people who look after the car park at your hospital. Last Thursday I returned to my car after visiting my sister who is a long-term patient in your cardiac unit, to discover that it had been clamped. There was an Ace Parking van nearby (clearly the people who had done the clamping) and I remonstrated with the two men who were in the van. I had placed my pay and display ticket in the window of my car as usual and I insisted that they had made a mistake. I thought I was well within my three hour parking time.

Unknown to me you have recently increased your car park charges and while they explained this to me the way in which they did it was rude and inconsiderate. I admit that I was upset, I needed to get back to work, but the way they spoke to me was unacceptable. They told me to 'use my eyes' (pointing to the parking charge increase notice) and, when I argued, told me to 'get a life'. This is not acceptable.

Since then I have spoken to three other hospital visitors who were clamped on the same day and they told me that they had received rude and inconsiderate treatment as well. I can happily provide you with their names.

As well as a full apology I want the fine of £30 refunded and, more importantly, I want an assurance that this will not happen again. Surely you must realise that people using your parking are often in a hurry, sometimes distressed and often elderly. To be treated this way for an honest mistake only two days after you had increased your charges is disgusting. I have copied this letter to my MP, to the Southern Press newspaper and to the Hospital Visitors Association.

I look forward to hearing from you.

S Hopkins

ITEM 5

Email

From: Bill Wayne: Head of Site Services

To: Chris Jenner

Date: 12/10/2015

Unit No.	Accomm	Status	From	Until	Notes
1,2,3,4,5	3 Bed	Let	1/1/2014	1/1/2016	All in good condition, next refurbishment in 2017
6,7	3 Bed	Let	1/1/2014	1/11/2015	In poor condition, plumbing in urgent need of maintenance and decoration also poor
8,9	2 Bed	Available			Maintenance completed on 1.10.2015
10	4 Bed	Let	1/8/2015	1/12/2015	Average condition, next refurbishment due 1.5.2016
11	Large 3 Bed	Let	1/12/2013	1/1/2017	Good condition
12	2 Bed	Let	1/12/2014	1/1/2016	Good condition

Hi Chris, here are those figures you asked for.

ITEM 6

Email

From: Dr R Ahmad: Head of Accident and Emergency

To: Chris Jenner

Date: 14/10/2015

Dear Chris

I spoke with you on Thursday about the repairs to the roof canopy above the A&E admissions bay. The scaffolding is still up and this is causing a problem for the ambulance drivers who cannot pull up immediately outside the doors. I thought you said that the scaffolding would be down by today?

Can you get on to the contractors immediately – I think it is South West Roofing? It only needs one incident with several admissions and the ambulances will be backed up into the car park!

Raj

ITEM 7

Phone message

15/10/2015

Hi Chris

I took a phone message early this morning from a Mr Paul Anderson from Ace Parking. He wants an urgent meeting about their contract because he has heard rumours that we might be going to cancel their contract; I think someone from the newspapers has been in touch! He sounded quite upset so I think someone had better get back to him.

Ceri

Admin secretary

ITEM 8

Email

From: Phil Weston: Contracts Manager South West Roofing

To: Chris Jenner

Date: 14/10/2015

Dear Chris

Thank you for your message. As I explained at the site meeting last week, the problem with the scaffolding is that we subcontracted this work and the firm we used has now gone into receivership. As you know we have completed our work but we are unable to contact anyone at the scaffolders to get them to remove the two remaining scaffold towers.

Sorry about this. I am chasing them every day but there is not much we can do until we can find out who is in charge of the company. Everyone seems to be passing the buck at the moment.

Phil Weston

ITEM 9

Email

From: Ian Hopkin: Manager Patient Relations

To: Chris Jenner

Date: 14/10/2015

Hi Chris, here are the results from the last patient satisfaction survey, I think they make quite good reading and when you get the chance I'd like to discuss with you options for using the information.

Cheers

Ian

Patient survey results September 2015
Total responses = 1620

Question	Mean response (7 point scale where 7 is high)	Change + or − on last year	Outpatients	Inpatients
I am happy with the level of service I have received	5.2	+0.2	5.0	5.4
I had access to all the information I needed	4.8	+0.4	5.2	5.0
Staff were always responsive and supportive	5.8	+0.3	5.4	5.9
I am satisfied with hospital cleanliness and hygiene	4.3	−0.1	3.9	4.5
All processes and procedures were fully explained to me	4.0	−0.3	3.8	4.2
I am satisfied with my overall experience of the hospital	4.9	+0.3	4.9	4.9

How to respond

How did you get on? This section will enable you to compare your response to the exercise with a worked through answer.

If you remember the advice given earlier (page 141), then you will know that you should spend at least ten minutes getting an overview of the items, clustering them and then deciding how best to respond. Let's take this approach to these items.

Clustering: Items 1, 3 and 5 all relate to the same issue: accommodation
Items 2, 4 and 7 all relate to car parking issues
Items 6 and 8 relate to the A&E scaffolding issue
Item 9 is a separate document providing information

Hopefully this clustering makes the task look a little less daunting. The challenge now is to decide how to respond bearing in mind what I said about recognising the difference between issues which are urgent and those that are important. I will take each issue in turn. It is worth pointing out that what I describe below is not meant to be a 'perfect' answer: there will be many acceptable ways of tackling the issues. What the responses suggested do provide is comprehensive coverage of the problems.

Accommodation issue

Item 1: from this it is clear that a promise of suitable accommodation has been made to a new doctor who is expecting to move in tomorrow! It is always important to note dates and times in these exercises; you can't decide what is urgent otherwise!

Items 3 and 5: from these it is clear that there is a problem with the promised accommodation. From the information in item 5 it looks as though the most suitable accommodation (unit 6 or 7) is in poor condition. The only other suitable accommodation is unit 10 which is not available for another six weeks.

Item 3 also raises a longer term issue about the budget.

Response

So, what would a decent set of responses to these issues look like?

The most urgent problem is that the new doctor and his family are expecting somewhere to live when they arrive tomorrow. You only have two real options: let them have the substandard accommodation with a promise that they will be able to move into something better in six weeks (unit 10) or, say that no accommodation is available. Either way you need to start communicating now! In trays often present you with dilemmas that force you to make 'least bad' decisions and this is just such an example. Leaving Dr Okufee and his family on the street is probably the worst of these options so now you just have to respond appropriately and communicate this decision. What will your output have to include?

- An email to Dr Kennet explaining the problem. You will need to point out that you only recently became aware that there was a problem and that the accommodation will only be temporary until a better flat is available. A nice touch would also be to make an offer of getting in touch with Dr Okufee yourself to explain what is happening. This shows that you are taking responsibility and that you are alert to the importance of speedy communication in this situation.
- An email to Bill Wayne explaining the decision. It is probably also worth asking him if there is anything that can be done urgently to improve the accommodation. Again the tone of the email will be important, explaining that the problem has arisen quickly, that there is no alternative other than to let Okufee have unit 6 or 7 and that you really appreciate any help he can provide.
- A response to the budget issue. Bill Wayne needs to know that you have recognised his concern and that you are going to take action. You might include this response as part of the above email or do it as a separate message. A sensible response would be to ask for a meeting with him to discuss and better understand the budget issue. You could also write an email asking for time at the next finance committee meeting to discuss the accommodation budget: this would clearly tell the assessors that you have recognised the longer-term issue but that you are producing a measured response rather than raising concerns before you have all the relevant information.

The actual messages might look something like this.

Letter to Dr Kennet

Dear Dr Kennet

My apologies for letting you know this at such short notice but I have to raise an issue about the accommodation for Dr Okufee. I have only been made aware of this issue myself this morning but I felt it important to keep you informed. The units which were to be made available to Dr Okufee are in urgent need of refurbishing, I understand they are perfectly habitable but in need of some work. My best suggestion is that Dr Okufee occupies one of these units in the short term and I am ensuring that a better and larger flat will be available for him and his family from early in December. I apologise again for any embarrassment this causes you: if you like I would be happy to get in touch with Dr Okufee myself if this helps. I will keep you informed of progress.

Yours

Letter to Bill Wayne

Dear Bill

I have taken over from Chris Jenner at very short notice this morning and I wanted to raise a couple of urgent matters that I have found in Chris's in tray. I saw your message about units 6 and 7 being in need of urgent refurbishment, however we have made a prior commitment to a new doctor and his family who are expecting to move in tomorrow. I apologise that you had not been made aware of this but at this short notice I think our hands are tied. Any help you can offer in terms of preparing one of these units would be much appreciated. I'm going to suggest that this accommodation is only for six weeks until unit 10 becomes available if this is alright with you?

I would also appreciate a meeting with you ASAP, it would be good to have the chance to introduce myself and to hear from you about the accommodation budget situation before I take your concerns to the finance committee. Looking forward to working with you.

Yours

Letter to admin secretary

Could you please let me know the date for the next finance committee meeting and find out if it is possible for me to add a discussion of the accommodation budget to the agenda for that meeting?

Yours

KEEP IT REAL

It is important to respond in as realistic a way as you can to in-tray items. The more complete you can make your messages the better. It doesn't mean that every response has to be a long one but try to cover all the bases in terms of producing a complete and polite email or letter. Assessors will respond much better to these than to your notes explaining what you would do: far better to show them as full a response as you can manage in the time.

Parking issue

Item 2: this lets you know that there has been a history of disquiet about hospital parking, the final comment about not being able to get a response is one that you might want to respond to if you have time.

Item 4: a message from an unhappy customer, and potentially an influential one. Clearly you will want to respond to her, the issue will be how fully you can respond in the available time.

Item 7: a message from Ace Parking: it seems likely that Miss Hopkins has contacted the press and that they have tried to contact Paul Anderson hence his state of concern.

Response

None of these items has a pressing deadline but they all represent situations that will get worse if you do not take action. There may also be a more systemic problem with Ace Parking that needs to be dealt with and a public relations problem. Assessors marking an in-tray exercise will be impressed if you show that you are willing to make some progress in tackling this kind of non-crisis issue.

Your response should include the following items.

- A letter to Miss Hopkins: given how little you know about the situation, a well worded holding letter is probably the most appropriate response, promising that you will investigate and then get back to her.
- A letter or email to Paul Anderson asking for an urgent meeting to sort out the car parking issues and to clarify the rumours. As far as you are aware no decision has been made about the parking contract but this is a good time to discuss the service they are providing in the light of complaints.
- A note or a meeting request in order to look at the car parking issues more broadly. It is not clear from the information you have who would be the appropriate attendees of this meeting but you have enough information to tell you that it is having a negative impact on hospital PR. It makes sense then to flag up that you have recognised it as an issue and a short note will tell the assessors this.

A&E scaffolding issue

Item 6: clearly this raises a concern that you have to deal with; it has a potential impact on patient care. Assessors will want to see that you are treating this as an urgent item.

Item 8: an explanation of why the scaffolding is still up but it is distinctly unhelpful in resolving the problem. This is a good example of the kind of item that is put into an in tray in order to assess your ability or willingness to 'make things happen' so the action you take will be important.

Response

Your response should include the following.

- An urgent email to Dr Ahmad explaining the problem but, most importantly, that you are on top of the issue and are going to do something about it. The options you might consider are:
  - pressing the contractor to remove the scaffolding themselves regardless of the subcontractor issue
  - getting a third party firm to remove the scaffolding and worry about who will pay for it later
  - find out if hospital maintenance has the resource to take down the scaffolding

■ An urgent email requesting a meeting, today if possible as this shows you recognise the urgency, with Phil Weston to find ways of getting the scaffolding removed.

Patient satisfaction survey

Item 9: information regarding the results of a patient survey. This does not seem to need any urgent response. For the sake of politeness and completeness it would be wise to respond to Ian Hopkin acknowledging receipt of the information, agreeing that the results look good and accepting the offer of a meeting.

If you have time, a really strong response might include noting that outpatients have slightly lower ratings than inpatients and suggesting that reasons for this would be worth discussion with the relevant department heads.

As you can see from the above examples, a lot of the secret in handling in-tray exercises/case studies well is to organise yourself, to prioritise and to get the timing right. It is generally better to produce at least some response to all the important issues rather than leave something out entirely. If you do leave something out or ignore it because you don't feel it is important, it is worth adding a note that you have done this deliberately, otherwise the assessors have no way of telling if you ran out of time or if you just failed to recognise the issue as important.

The tips and guidance given above should help you to ensure that you let your abilities shine through despite the inevitable time pressure that these exercises create.

Relationship to competencies

Here are some typical competencies, together with the behavioural indicators, that assessors would be likely to be looking for in an in-tray exercise. As I mentioned earlier (page 139), because assessors actually have written output to base their assessment on and are not constrained by the challenges of observing a 'live' exercise, it is quite common for in-tray/case study exercises to be assessing more competencies than other kinds of exercise.

Competency	Indicators for this exercise
Influencing and persuading	• Presents decisions with conviction • Builds a clear argument with a supporting rationale • Shows that the viewpoint of all relevant stakeholders has been considered • Anticipates difficult influencing challenges as part of the presentation, e.g. response to Miss Hopkins • The tone and style of letters/emails is appropriate to the recipient
Analytical thinking	• Identifies all the key issues and spots any relationships between them • Presents options and alternatives and not just one solution • Shows they have considered fall back options and has anticipated challenges • Shows evidence of having prioritised
Planning and organising	• Covers all the issues, nothing is missed out • Produces substantive responses to all items requiring a response • Output in the form of letters or emails are well structured and clear
Judgement and decision making	• Takes action on items, does not defer all decisions • Responses are well thought through in terms of impact, tone and the likelihood of them progressing the issue • Decisions are justifiable based on the available information; any assumptions are made clear. Responses show that the items have been considered holistically

Additional pointers for case study and analytical exercises

Case study exercises share many of the characteristics of in trays and the key pointers to success are the same. There are a few additional points to bear in mind, however.

Case studies are usually subject specific, they assume that you have some specific knowledge about a topic that the assessors want to test. For this reason it is not practical to illustrate the vast range of subject matter that could come up. The assessment could be seeking to test your knowledge across anything from the housing market to quality control. Remember that you will only be given this kind of exercise if you have applied for a job where this background knowledge and experience was a clear requirement.

In a case study you will usually be given a sheaf of material relating to the subject matter and then asked to do something with it. This will usually take one or all of the following forms:

■ provide your analysis of the issues or challenges contained in the material
■ make a decision about the best course of action based on the material
■ make recommendations.

You may recognise this kind of required output from the section on presentations in Chapter 7. After all, the case study is simply asking you to put into writing the same kind of material that you would be asked to cover in a presentation.

Structure

You will usually be given very clear guidelines as to the expected structure of your output for any case study you experience because an assessor will have to mark it and they usually have limited time. Following the guidelines is important: if you produce a rambling essay rather than the clear bullet points they have asked for then you will not be doing yourself any favours. A typical structure would be as follows:

■ identify key issues
■ evaluate a range of options
■ justify the options you have selected
■ make a clear recommendation.

Even in the limited time you will have available, it pays to try and build an argument rather than just provide terse notes: a clear structure with headings will help you to achieve this.

Planning

In an assessment centre you will have limited time to complete any case study exercise and furthermore, this time might well be split across different sessions. It is important, therefore, to plan how you are going to use your time; for example how much time you will devote to reading the material and then how much for actually writing your response. Make sure you give enough time to the recommendations section; this will usually come at the end of your output and you need to give yourself time to complete it.

Breadth vs depth

Depending on the level of job you are applying for, a case study exercise will be trying to get at the breadth as well as the depth of your knowledge about whatever the relevant subject matter is. It is very easy to get 'lost' in the detail of the material that they have given you, focusing on the analytical element of the exercise at the expense of bringing in your own knowledge and experience. Make sure you give yourself time to 'add value' to the case study by bringing in your own expertise. In the end this is what will differentiate you from other candidates, as most candidates will do a half decent job of analysing the material that has been provided.

Don't sit on the fence!

If you are asked for recommendations, then make recommendations! Assessors will quickly become frustrated by case study output that covers all the relevant options but then fails to suggest what should happen. A key competency that most case study exercises will be evaluating is your judgement in relation to a particular area of expertise. If you make no recommendations then the assessors have no way of evaluating your judgement, and they will not give you the benefit of the doubt. Clearly there are some dangers in getting it 'wrong' in the sense that the recommendations just don't make sense (though I'm sure yours will!): so by all means offer caveats and fall-back options but not at the expense of making your view about the best course of action clear.

As with all other assessment centre exercises, a subject matter specific case study will be assessing more than one competency, more than just your technical knowledge in a particular area. As before then, think about this kind of exercise holistically.

IN A NUTSHELL

■ In trays, case studies and analytical exercises all try and simulate the task of sifting through material and then responding appropriately by writing letters, a report or communicating decisions.

■ The key to doing well is managing your time to make sure that you deal with appropriate detail as well as with the bigger picture.

■ Remember to read all the items to get an overview.

■ Prioritise what is urgent and what is important and allocate your time effectively

■ Make your responses, for example the letters or emails you write, 'real' and fit for purpose, not just rough notes.

■ Look for underlying systemic issues as well as the ones that leap out from the items.

■ In case studies and in trays, let your experience 'add value' to your output rather than just treating the exercise as an analytical task.

9 TROUBLESHOOTING

This chapter will focus on some of the questions that arise most frequently from people who are attending an assessment centre as well as trying to dispel some of the common misconceptions about how to perform well at an assessment centre. It will include:

- questions about general approach

- questions about specific exercises.

Frequently asked questions

If I do badly at an assessment centre will I get the chance to explain why?

It is good practice for the company you are applying to to provide you with feedback after the assessment centre, though any explanations you provide at this point will be unlikely to change the result. Some assessment centres do allow for de-brief time at the end of every exercise, but while this gives you some scope to explain your performance, it is unlikely to change how you have been scored.

EXERCISE DEBRIEF

In some assessment centres there is time built in to de-brief at the end of each exercise. Use this time well to get feedback and to get clues about what assessors are looking for. If you are asked for your view about how a particular exercise went, then be as objective as you can. Assessors will want to see that you show self-awareness and that you can objectively evaluate your own performance.

Will allowances and reasonable adjustments be made if I have any disabilities which I think might affect my performance?

Yes, most employers will recognise their obligation to make reasonable adjustments. Make sure that you flag up any concerns you have well in advance of the centre. As the head of recruitment at a government department has emphasised to us: 'Our priority is recruiting the best people for the job and our selection process should not be a barrier for candidates with disabilities. We actively encourage our candidates to get in touch if they need to discuss any adjustments.'

Will I be competing with the other candidates I meet at the assessment centre?

It is best not to think of the assessment centre as a competition. Rarely will you be competing for only one job. Often several candidates, as long as they meet the standard, will be accepted as a result of the assessment. Focus on your own performance rather than how you think other candidates are doing.

How should I behave in an open ended group discussion exercise if someone else in the group has obviously taken the lead?

Don't try to compete inappropriately for leadership of the group (especially if the person who has taken the lead seems to be doing a reasonable job) but do make sure that your voice is heard and that you don't just 'go along' with a discussion that is heading in the wrong direction. Assessors will penalise the group leader if they are doing a poor job but they will also take note if you don't try to do something about it!

What should I do if another candidate is being difficult or disruptive during a group meeting exercise?

The first thing to say is that such behaviour will go down very badly with the assessors but it is important that you don't allow it to put you off or let it lead to a poor discussion which might affect how your own performance is rated. The assessors will be impressed if you are able to calmly and objectively deal with the disruptive behaviour without letting it get personal. It is much better to deal with the behaviour rather than let it spoil the discussion. Be brave and ask the person why they are behaving in that way and what can the group do to help. Ignoring the behaviour will leave the assessors doubting your ability to assert yourself appropriately.

FEEDBACK

Regardless of the circumstances in which you encounter an assessment centre, make sure you get feedback. The assessment centre will have given the organisation valuable information about where your skills and attributes match their needs: it makes sense for you to benefit from this information as well so that you can hone your performance or enhance your experience.

I'm no good at acting; will this put me at a disadvantage in role play exercises?

Yes – so don't act! All that is required is that you imagine yourself to be in the situation described, be yourself and follow the advice in Chapter 6. This is not acting – you do it every time you meet someone new. If you suspect that this kind of exercise will make you particularly nervous then use the examples in Chapter 6 to practise – give the role player's brief to a friend or colleague and simulate the exercise.

I'm worried that being good at assessment centres is all about how extraverted and sociable you are. I'm fairly reserved, will this put me at a disadvantage?

In a well-designed assessment centre the assessors will be looking at a wide range of attributes not just how socially confident you are. This said you do need to ensure that you contribute during interactive exercises and the advice in the previous chapters will help. It is not helpful to get into a mindset that says you find this kind of exercise 'difficult'. Rather, think about specific behaviours that will help or hinder in specific situations and practise using them or avoiding them. For example, if the issue is that you are quite reserved and find it difficult to speak up during group discussions, then stop focusing on 'being reserved' and start focusing on specific phrases, questions or observations you can practise and use to get your voice heard. You can change your behaviour, you are unlikely to change your personality so don't talk yourself into a negative mindset.

If I think I have done particularly poorly in an exercise will I have blown my chances?

No! So it is important to put a bad exercise behind you and focus on the opportunities provided by the next exercise. Very few people perform uniformly well across all assessment centre exercises, that is why the relevant competencies are measured more than once across different situations. Assessment centres try to recognise that any individual's strengths can show up in different ways in different situations. So don't get disheartened by what you think is a poor exercise.

Will an assessment centre test my technical knowledge?

Some assessment centres will contain an exercise (usually a case study) designed to evaluate your breadth of knowledge/experience in a specific area that is relevant to the job. This will only be one element of the assessment, however, and most of the exercise will be looking at a much broader range of your job relevant skills.

Who are the assessors on an assessment centre?

The assessors will usually be people who already work for the organisation, usually one or two levels more senior than the post you are applying for, and often they will be supported by assessment specialists such as business psychologists. They will all have been trained in using competencies and behavioural indicators as a way of coming to an objective evaluation of your performance.

10 AND FINALLY...

Experience of hundreds of assessment centres and thousands of candidates makes it clear that practice and preparation makes a huge difference to how well people perform during this kind of selection process. Yes, there are some people out there who can just 'wing it' and still perform well but this isn't true of most of us.

Preparation and practice is particularly important if you are about to experience your first assessment centre but it is also highly valuable to people who have been through a number of assessment centres and just can't quite put their finger on why they seem to fail them. The insights provided by this book, particularly those related to seeing the process from the assessor's point of view, will make a big difference to your performance.

At the outset I said that an assessment centre can seem to be a very daunting experience – hopefully I have demystified the process. I also said that the best way of looking at an assessment centre is as a number of different opportunities to show your prospective employer what you can do. This book should have helped you to make the most of those opportunities.

In my experience a little preparation and practice is worth a ton of soul searching after the event; understanding the nuts and bolts of an assessment centre will really make that preparation and practice pay off.

Good luck!
Ceri Roderick

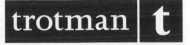